MW00655273

"If you love your family and want your children and their children to be contributors to society rather than merely consumers, *The Gift of Lift* is must-read. It is an insightful and even inspiring guide full of important information and ideas on how you can elevate future generations. I love the book and will be recommending it to everyone who loves their family and wants to create a lasting legacy of caring and capable heirs."

—Lee M. Brower, Founder of Empowered Wealth, LC,
   Author, Speaker


"*The Gift of Lift* is a powerful book that shows us how to find purpose and meaning in our lives. Through the author's journey and multiple stories from incredible stewards across human history, David demonstrates how we can create a more fulfilling life by investing in something bigger than ourselves. This book is perfect for anyone looking to create a more challenging and rewarding path in their life, their family, and their business, driven by purpose and lasting impact. In the end, David also provides a valuable how-to guide to find your own stewardship journey."

—Juana Catalina Rodriguez, Founder and CEO, JnC Nova,
   Author of *Unsettled Disruption*


"*The Gift of Lift* beautifully and articulately lays out the difference between ownership and stewardship, a key distinction for any for-profit (or even non-profit) enterprise and one sorely missing from our culture today. Using the language of values and virtues from ancient to modern times, David inspires the reader to identify, articulate, and lead with purpose."

—John Montgomery, Founder, Bridgeway Capital Management
   and Bridgeway Foundation

"David's legacy will not be because of any mastery of estate planning (though make no mistake, he is a master). Rather, his will be one of stewardship—not of wealth but of people—as he has dedicated his passion and pursuits to teaching and inspiring countless others to lead lives of greater intentionality and impact for the benefit of those around them. *The Gift of Lift* is a simple yet profound treatise on just that—how to positively impact the people around us, irrespective of the resources we may (or may not) have at our disposal. One comes away feeling both uplifted and resolute in quietly leading a life of greater purpose in service to others."

—Chris Klomp, Tech Entrepreneur

"What a wonderful and inspiring book. David has provided readers in all cultures with a road map for becoming a steward—someone with a transcendent purpose who is 'all in.' The world needs all the stewards the Divine can provide!"

—Fred Kiel, Author of *Return on Character*

"*The Gift of Lift* is an amazing journey into what is truly important in your life and your family. Although it is a dynamic delve into the concept of 'stewardship,' as I read, I couldn't help critically examining my own priorities and how to better influence my own family values. It is a must-read for anyone interested in holistic family planning."

—Andrew L. Howell, Esq., Estate Planning Attorney, Co-Author of *Entrusted: Building a Legacy that Lasts*

"I have been advising multigenerational families for nearly twenty-five years. When I moved to Ronald Blue Trust to help build out the firm's Family Office division, one our early initiatives was to incorporate the principles set out in David's first book, *Entrusted: Building a Legacy that Lasts.* The lessons of that book were so thoughtful and clearly explained we have practically made it required reading for new hires within the Family Office. In his latest book, *The Gift of Lift*, he has done it again. One of the most powerful life lessons we can teach next-generation family members is that they are healthier, happier, and more fulfilled when they pursue a life of purpose and meaning. This book does an excellent job illustrating the difference between pursuing happiness versus purpose. This too will likely become required reading."

**—Skip Perkins, Ronald Blue Trust, Family Office Division**

"David does an excellent job examining and demonstrating the power of stewardship. His research for this work was exceptional, and his examples are spot-on. Those seeking to make a greater, positive impact in our families and communities should read this book."

**—John H. Nebeker, LUTCF®, CLTC®, CASL®, Nebeker Financial Services, Inc.**

*The Gift of Lift:*
*Harnessing the Power of Stewardship to Elevate the World*

by David R. York

ISBN 978-1-64663-663-1

Published by

**köehlerbooks**™

3705 Shore Drive
Virginia Beach, VA 23455
800-435-4811
www.koehlerbooks.com

# THE GIFT OF LIFT

## Harnessing the Power of Stewardship to Elevate the World

# DAVID R. YORK

VIRGINIA BEACH
CAPE CHARLES

To hear never-heard sounds,
To see never-seen colors and shapes,
To try to understand the imperceptible
Power pervading the world;
To fly and find pure ethereal substances
That are not of matter
But of that invisible soul pervading reality.
To hear another soul and to whisper to another soul;
To be a lantern in the darkness
Or an umbrella in a stormy day;
To feel much more than know.
To be the eyes of an eagle, slope of a mountain;
To be a wave understanding the influence of the moon;
To be a tree and read the memory of the leaves;
To be an insignificant pedestrian on the streets
Of crazy cities watching, watching, and watching.
To be a smile on the face of a woman
And shine in her memory
As a moment saved without planning.

**—Dejan Stojanovic**

To my wife, Melinda, and my children,
Emma, John, Samuel, Hudson, and Avery.
You are truly the greatest gifts and the reason for lift in my life.

# TABLE OF CONTENTS

# Author's Note

At the age of forty-nine, while waking up slowly in a quiet hotel room at the beginning of a hot and humid family vacation, I read three words on my computer screen that brought instant shock, confusion, and bewilderment:

*Predicted Relationship: Father.*

Next to those words were the profile picture of someone I did not recognize and a name I did not know. It certainly was not the face or name of my father, who had passed away four years earlier. I was a York from Kentucky, the first to be born in a hospital and the second to go to college. I was the son of a man who grew up in poverty and became a successful self-made entrepreneur, who chose to become a CPA instead of following his dream of playing in a band because he knew that life would be incompatible with providing for a family. A man who served his country as a sailor and who loved its flag.

At least that was the story I'd been told. A year or so earlier, I had sent off a saliva sample to 23andMe, without having the slightest clue about the family secrets it contained. That morning I logged back in to check out some new information that had been added to my profile, when I suddenly and unceremoniously joined the ranks of the NPE: Not Parent Expected. Estimates are that between 3 and 5 percent of those who check into their genetics discover that their DNA tells a story that is different from the one they had been told.

I suddenly felt unmoored and disconnected, as if the strings that had always held me in place from above had been cut. Who was I? Where did I come from? If I didn't know this one little fact about my life, what else didn't I know? Who else knew the truth? Was everyone in on the secret but me? In the span of thirty seconds, I went from blissful ignorance to complete uncertainty.

In many respects, all that I knew about my father still held true. He had always treated me as his own—which was what made the information in front of me all the more unsettling. In the days that followed, I came to learn that my parents had struggled to have a child and had taken advantage of the fertility options available to them at the time, which had included a fill-in for half of my DNA. Had modern science in the form of a genetic website not intervened, my parents' decision would have gone on unknown. After my birth, they had apparently never really discussed the fact that I was not biologically my father's child and hadn't told anyone.

The first emotion I felt, after recovering from the shock, was one of overwhelming joy. Not because my dad was not my father. Quite the opposite. You see, in addition to two biological children, my wife and I also have three adopted children. In that moment, I felt a powerful realization that biology means nothing and that my dad was . . . my dad—the person I walk like, talk like, and crack jokes like. In that instant, I felt a kinship with my adopted children and experienced the feeling I hope and trust they share, which is that their dad *is* their dad.

The revelation of my genetics caused me to question many things and, like a dramatic twist in a movie, led me to replay much of my life in light of this new information. I understand now why I don't look like my father or his side of the family, where the red hair and freckles came from, and so many other tiny unexplainables (like the fact that I was short and chubby and my brother, who was biologically my father's son, was tall and skinny) that had, to that point in life, given me little pause. That said, after seeing those three words, "Predicted Relationship: Father," I also knew two things were fundamentally true:

1. Your family is the people you love and who love you in return.
2. The quality of your family is equal to the quality of that love.

Regardless of our genetic coding, our heritage, the color of our skin, or any of the other myriad differences that make us wonderfully different and powerfully the same, we all have a foundational need for a family to love and to love us in return. Truly now more than ever, we need to move beyond the notion that family is dictated merely by one's circumstances, genes, or biology. We need to embrace a far more expansive view of family that includes our friends, coworkers, employees, blended families, faith communities, and neighbors. So many of us struggle with difficult biological family situations or feel alone in this orphan-filled world, and yet none of us can fully live without the love of family. And so, it's time to reimagine what the word "family" really means and to shed the restrictive constructs that keep us from caring for and investing in one another, as family is meant to do.

In the pages that follow, I will lay out a different way of looking at and living life, one that is based in intentionality and connectedness. As you read this book, my hope is that you will embrace a more expansive view of your circle of influence and who your family really is or potentially could be. The life and mindset of a steward is a deeply others-centered approach to life that is built on all-out love and rooted in investment and relationship. My hope is that this book inspires you to embrace the life of a steward and to fully engage in the lives of those around you through your words, through your thoughts, and through your actions.

# About the Title

*"The desire to fly is an idea handed down to us by our
ancestors who, in their grueling travels across trackless
lands in prehistoric times, looked enviously on the birds
soaring freely through space, at full speed, above all obstacles,
on the infinite highway of the air."*

**—Wilbur Wright**

On December 17, 1903, Orville Wright climbed into Wright Flyer and made history with a twelve-second takeoff that covered 120 feet, becoming the first person to experience powered flight. Orville and his brother, Wilbur, learned about flight by watching birds and mimicking the look, feel, and design of their wings. In the nearly 120 years since, there have been staggering advancements in the field of aviation. Powered gliders morphed into airplanes, jets, and eventually spacecraft. While knowledge about aerodynamics and its otherworldly compatriot, astrodynamics, has grown logarithmically, scientists and engineers are still not exactly sure why and how a plane actually takes off from the ground.

What is known is that there are four primary forces that act to create flight: thrust (the force that propels the plane forward), drag (the force that works against thrust), weight (the force that keeps the plane on the ground), and lift (the force that raises the plane up). There are two general theories as to why *lift* exists and acts to create flight. The first, as we may recall from high school science, is what is commonly known as the Bernoulli principle. Bernoulli was an eighteenth-century scientist who studied fluid dynamics, which included both liquid and air. He correctly theorized that the pressure of a fluid decreases as its velocity increases, and, because of the curvature of the top of a wing (known as the airfoil), air traveling over the top of the wing moves faster than the air moving along the wing's bottom surface, thereby creating low pressure above the wing and high pressure below the wing, resulting in the upward force of lift.

The only problem with Bernoulli's principle is that it isn't correct, at least not entirely. One of the assumptions on which the principle is based is the idea that the air traveling over the wing must go faster to "catch up" with the air below, but in fact that air above the wing goes slightly faster than the air below, even though it travels a farther distance. The principle also doesn't explain why planes can fly upside down because the inverted wings should act in an opposite manner and force the plane down, but they don't.

The incorrect assumptions that undergird the principle led to a second theory, based on Newton's third law. This theory is based on the fact that air has mass and says that the wings' downward push of air passing under the wing results in an equal and opposite pushback along the bottom of the wing. This would solve the problem of planes flying upside down, but still doesn't explain why there is a low-pressure zone above the wing when it should be the opposite.[1]

Regardless of whether one of these two theories is the correct one, or whether it's some combination of the two (or even a yet-to-be discovered answer), the reality is that humanity has greatly advanced because of the upward force of lift. It has been used to connect cultures, bridge divides, advance science, ferry resources around the globe, and generally make this great big world a little bit smaller.

Like planes in our physical world, lift is also a mysterious yet powerful metaphysical force in the lives of those women and men who themselves combine a steadfast forward momentum with an eye bent toward the horizon. It allows those who take to the sky above to overcome the weights of the world, some self-imposed and others bestowed by fate, that can hold us down and instead soar above their circumstances. For the select few who dare to lighten their load and reach out their arms to embrace something far grander, the gift of lift allows them to go where few ultimately tread, allowing them to see the beauty of perspective and the blessings that ground dwellers rarely ever experience—freedom, clarity, and vision.

# Introduction

In 1985, Larry Miller was a successful businessman with a growing automobile sales business, raising five children with his wife, Gail, in Salt Lake City, Utah. He had recently acquired another dealership and was thoroughly immersed in the challenges of running those business operations and becoming an accomplished entrepreneur. The last thing on his mind was owning a professional sports franchise.

The Utah Jazz was a financially strapped National Basketball Association team trying desperately to stay afloat in the smallest market in the league. The Jazz had joined the NBA in 1974 as an expansion team but had moved from New Orleans to Utah in 1979 after failing to make a go of it in the Big Easy. Unfortunately, the Jazz did not fare much better financially in Utah and had even traded away the draft rights to Dominique Wilkins in 1982 just to bring the team enough money to continue operating.

In February of 1985, while going through his mail, Miller found an unsolicited information packet on the Jazz that had been sent to various business leaders in the community, seeking investors in the struggling franchise. At the time, the busy Millers had never even been to a Utah Jazz game. But something about the organization caught Larry's attention. He and his wife started looking into the Jazz and came to realize that the team was a vitally important community asset, which, if lost, would never return to the state. Within two months, Larry and Gail went from non-attenders to half-owners of the team. Doing so required them to take on debt that was double their net worth—all to acquire a business that had not only never made a profit but had also lost $1 million or more every year of its eleven years in the league. The year after their first investment, the Millers bought the remaining 50 percent of the Jazz to ensure that they stayed in Utah and became the team's full owners.

A little over thirty years later, I sat across from Gail, working on the final details of a transfer of her ownership in the Jazz to a special trust she was establishing for the sole purpose of ensuring the Jazz stayed in the Salt Lake community. Since the Millers' acquisition of the team, Larry had passed away, and the Jazz had become not just an incredibly successful team—on the court and off—but, in many ways, had also become one of the most important fixtures in the state. The franchise had also paid off financially. Still located in one of the smallest markets in the NBA, the Jazz organization had nonetheless acquired tremendous value, not only because of its strong economic moat (there are only thirty such franchises in existence) but also because of its growing worth to potential buyers who might seek to move it to a larger market.

The Jazz had been a labor of love for the Millers, who had invested millions of dollars and an untold amount of time in the team, because they'd viewed it as a vital asset to their community and state. After more than two years of negotiations with the NBA and countless hours of effort, all the pieces were in place, and we were nearing completion of the transfer of the team to the trust Gail had carefully designed, and we were getting ready to announce the move to the public.

Marveling at the amount of wealth Gail was planning on transferring to a trust that wouldn't provide her any personal benefit,

I asked her what I thought was a simple question, "Gail, does it bother you at all to give away your ownership in the Jazz?"

Gail looked up from the documents we were reviewing and said flatly, "I don't own the Utah Jazz."

Her response both surprised me and gave me pause. Not only is Gail Miller one of the sharpest and wisest clients I have ever had the opportunity to work with, but she is also an astute businesswoman who knows the key operating details of each of her more than eighty operating businesses.

"But you actually *do* own the Jazz," I replied a bit tentatively, making sure, as her estate planner, that she was one hundred percent clear about the facts at hand. I will never forget her response; it was one of the single most powerful moments of my entire professional career as an estate planning attorney.

"No. I don't," she replied, sitting back and looking me straight in the eye in a way that told me she knew exactly what she was saying and doing. "I'm a *steward* of the Jazz."

Her simple yet powerful reply has reverberated in my mind ever since and has launched me on a journey to understand what a steward is and how the concept of stewardship can lead someone like Gail to transcend a magnetic force as powerful as personal ownership, even when an asset with a potential billion-dollar value is involved.[2]

This book is my attempt at an answer.

*The Gift of Lift* is not a business book. It is not a self-help book, a memoir, a history, or a treatise on economics. This book is about a *perspective* we can all choose to adopt when engaging with the world around us. Stewardship is for anyone who chooses to embrace it. A businessperson can certainly become a steward, but so too can a teacher, a stay-at-home parent, a doctor, a student, a construction worker, or a public servant. Stewards are defined by their approach to life, not by their titles, wealth, or accomplishments. Although stewards share certain commonalities with one another, the *expression* of those commonalities are as unique and diverse as the people and cultures of this planet. Versed in the art and science of meaning, stewards operate in a different economy and with their own unique currencies. They don't trade in money, fame, power, or prestige like most of us. Instead, they fully invest themselves in purpose, passion, and, above all else, people. Their scorecards aren't made of balance sheets or organizational charts. Rather, they score themselves in how they impact their families, coworkers, and communities.

Besides simply operating with a different rubric for life, one of the other truly unique characteristics of stewards is that they do not buy into myriad myths about money, wealth, and happiness that are so prevalent in our world today. They see through these myths to the realities of life and, in doing do, they operate with a sense of clarity and purpose that is all too uncommon today. Throughout this book, I'll identify some of these popular myths and the realities that stewards see and understand.

As you read the pages that follow, my hope is that you will think about ways that *you* can break free of a life on the ground by fully investing in something bigger than yourself. My dream is for a world of women and men who look up and let go of the weights that drag them down and keep them in place and who instead press forward with such force and velocity that their outstretched arms lift them off and away to the realm of something more. My hope is that you let go of anything but your purpose so that you can feel the passion, freedom, and community engagement that marks the life of a steward.

# CHAPTER 1

# Building Blocks

*"Man must rise above the Earth—to the top of the*
*atmosphere and beyond—for only thus will he fully*
*understand the world in which he lives."*

**—Socrates**

Rome is the capital of Italy and the former hub of the Western world. In the fifth century BC, however, Rome was merely one of many city-states scattered across the planet and was still in its relative infancy. To the north, the Etruscans were a unique and insular civilization with a language and well-developed culture all their own. To the south, the Greeks had established multiple colonies throughout the southern half of the Italic Peninsula. Rome stood in the midst of various trade and travel routes between these groups, which rendered it a teeming metropolis for a wide range of people and perspectives. The last king of Rome had left the city on the heels of scandal in 509 BC, and the seeds of what would eventually become the Roman Republic had been planted in the place vacated by the deposed monarch.

The Republic—derived from the Latin term *res publica*, which literally means "public thing"—was the Romans' attempt to address the problems of concentrated power. It consisted of two councils appointed by a senate, which itself comprised two groups. The first group was made up of elder statesmen, known as the patricians, or fathers of Rome. The second group was drawn from the plebes, or "crowds," and consisted of wealthy and respected members of the community who had not attained the social status of a patrician. These two groups tussled for power for more than two centuries before any semblance of stability was attained.

It was during this time of change and upheaval that Lucius Quinctius Cincinnatus was born. Cincinnatus was a Roman statesman, farmer, and member of a prominent patrician family. In 460 BC, Rome was at war with the neighboring Aequi tribe, and things were not going well for the Romans. One of the leaders of the Roman plebes had been assassinated, and Rome was in turmoil as it faced the prospects of a bitter and costly military defeat. In desperation, the Roman Senate appointed Cincinnatus dictator of Rome, which gave him unlimited powers for six months to deal with the crisis at hand. Notified of the appointment while working his fields located outside the city, Cincinnatus promptly set down his plow, went to his home to don his official robe, and headed to Rome.

As dictator, Cincinnatus had unrivaled power. He quickly assembled an army and led Rome to a short, decisive, and altogether unexpected victory. After bringing the defeated Aequi leaders back to Rome for judgment, Cincinnatus stepped down from his post after a mere sixteen days in office. Although his position and success would have enabled him to retain power far beyond his initial term, he returned to his farm and continued his simple life of work and family.

At the age of eighty, Cincinnatus was called upon and named dictator of Rome yet again, this time to deal with a famine resulting from another power struggle between the patricians and the plebes. For a second time, Cincinnatus succeeded in averting disaster for the fledgling Republic, and once again, he stepped down, this time after only twenty-one days. As a result, Cincinnatus rose from the fertile fields of the Roman countryside and into its lore, becoming an enduring example of virtue, honor, humility, and noble leadership.[3]

More than 2,000 years later and 4,000 miles away, the echoes of Cincinnatus reverberated in the heart and mind of another farmer-turned-statesman. In 1775, George Washington was named the general and commander in chief of the Continental Army and charged with the task of leading a ragtag collection of state militias against the most powerful army in the eighteenth century. For eight years, Washington fought a mostly hopeless, unsuccessful campaign, with major successes coming only at the beginning and the end of what came to be known as the American Revolutionary War. The decentralized control of the fledgling colonies proved to be one of the banes of Washington's command and likely caused the war to last far longer than it should have lasted. Regardless, after Washington's victory over Cornwallis in October 1781 and the formal signing of the Treaty of Paris in 1783, Washington resigned his position as leader of the Army before the Continental Congress on December 23, 1783.

Addressing Congress for what Washington thought would be his last official act before retiring to his beloved Mount Vernon, he said, "Having now finished the work assigned me, I retire from the great theatre of action, and bidding an affectionate farewell to this august body under whose orders I have so long acted, I here offer my commission, and take my leave of all the employments of public life."

His resignation was seen as such an exception to the norm of holding on to power for life that a depiction of the scene, titled *General George Washington Resigning His Commission*, painted by John Trumbull, hangs in the rotunda of the Capitol building alongside other scenes of monumental civic importance, including *Declaration of Independence*.

Washington's actions were seen by many at the time to be an American reflection of the virtue and values of Cincinnatus. Washington thought as much himself and drew on the example of

Cincinnatus from his classical education for his own attitudes and actions. And like his Roman role model, Washington was called upon a second time, becoming the only unanimously elected president of the United States. While serving far longer than Cincinnatus, Washington nevertheless retired from that position after two terms and set a precedent for every future president.

What makes both of these men such remarkable historical figures is that their actions ran starkly counter to the culture and nature of their times. For most of human existence, and even to this day, individuals and groups have been defined by power: who has it and who doesn't.

## THE PULL OF POWER

The Peloponnesian War was a fifth-century BC conflict between Sparta and Athens. Caught between these two powers sat the tiny island of Melos, which sought to avoid trouble by opting for the path of neutrality. Athens, wanting both tribute and support, sent envoys to Melos to explain that neutrality was not an option and that the Melians, in essence, needed to pick a side. The Melians responded by appealing to a higher sense of virtue, saying it was wrong of Athens to make them choose. The reply of the Athenians was short and to the point: "You know as well as we do that right, as the world goes, is only in question between equals in power, *while the strong do what they can and the weak suffer what they must.*" In other words, in the eyes of the Athenians, right and wrong came into question only when power could not supply the answer.[4]

Under such a construct, the last thing you would want to do in a violent, chaotic world is to voluntarily give up power. And yet, that is exactly what both Cincinnatus and Washington did. They chose principle over power. In England, when King George III heard about Washington giving up his command, he remarked, "If [Washington] does that, he will be the greatest man in the world."[5]

Each of these men also gave up power in the prime of his life. Essentially, they went out on top, which is something people in positions of power rarely do. Washington, like Cincinnatus before him, voluntarily put himself "on a clock," resolving that he would be in power only for a set time and purpose, and when that time was up, his work was done. They were both able to look down the road and see the world without them.

## STEWARDS

The English word *steward* comes from the Old English *stiweard*, from *stig*, meaning "house or hall," and *weard* or "ward." The word eventually came to mean a person who oversees the affairs or property of someone else, typically for a prescribed time or while the actual owner is away. It has grown in recent years to encompass a mentality or approach toward very big things, like finances, communities, and the environment.

In the New Testament, Jesus tells the story of a master and three servants. The master, preparing to go on a long journey, calls in each of the servants, one at a time. To the first, he entrusts five talents, roughly the equivalent of a lifetime of wages for a servant. To the second, he entrusts two talents, or more than thirty years' wages. To the third, he entrusts one talent, which nevertheless still represents more than fifteen years of labor. All three servants know their master is a demanding employer and will one day return. Accordingly, the first two servants put their talents to use, investing them and doubling their respective amounts. The third servant, however, decides to not risk the loss of the talent. Instead, he buries his talent so he can safely give it back to the master upon his return.[*]

When the master does finally return, he commends the two servants who put their talents to good use, but he takes back the talent of the third servant, gives it to the first servant, and casts servant number three out of his house. While all three had knowledge and opportunity, the first two possessed an additional quality that made them respond to the situation in a fundamentally different way. They saw themselves as stewards of the master's wealth, not merely security guards and not simply holders of resources for their own benefit or protection.

Stories of stewards aren't limited to the annals of history and religion. One of Dr. Seuss's most famous books, *Horton Hears a Who!*, is a story of stewardship that centers on the sacrificial determination of an elephant named Horton. Convinced that a microscopic population is living on a speck of dust, Horton decides that these people need protection from harm, and that he must be the one to offer it. Horton places the speck on a clover and proceeds to endure scorn, abuse, and rejection from others, all because of a promise he makes to the tiny inhabitants: "'Of course,' Horton answered. 'Of course I will stick. I will stick by you small folks through thin and through thick!'"[7] Theodor Seuss Geisel wrote *Horton* in response to his own change of heart on an important issue. Initially anti-Japanese because of that country's actions in World War II, Geisel eventually visited the island nation and left with a conviction that anger and resentment were wrong, and that the United States owed a duty to peoples in the world who couldn't provide for themselves.

So, what do a Roman farmer, the general of a ragtag army, a pair of biblical servants, and a fictional elephant have in common? What are the essential building blocks for a mindset that sees personal responsibility in a way that includes a self-sacrificing duty to something bigger? In essence, what makes someone a steward?

## THE BUILDING BLOCKS OF STEWARDS

The Capurso Winery is a fifth-generation family vineyard on the outskirts of Verona, Italy. Founded in 1896, it sits on forty pristine acres nestled amid rolling green hills, not far from where Romeo and Juliet (allegedly) fell in love. Each year it produces about 20,000 bottles of wine from the best 20 percent of the grapes it grows, all handpicked by local vineyard workers who have harvested the land for decades. The remaining 80 percent of the grapes are sold to a larger winery and bottled under a different label. Capurso's motto is "*Ci mettiamo vita, coltiviamo viti, celebriamo vini*" ("We live lives, we cultivate vines, we celebrate wines").

When visiting the winery in 2019, I had the opportunity to tour the grounds and talk with the daughter of the owner. She is part of the fifth generation operating the winery and is raising the sixth generation on the property. Marveling at the scenery as well as the longevity of these family vineyards, I asked her, "So, what is the secret of a five-generation business?"

She looked at me, thought for a moment, and said, "It is one word."

My mind raced through all the possible catchwords she might toss out: family, vision, commitment, profit, excellence, quality, wine (alcohol).

She then said, "The secret is *passion*. It is a beautiful work, but it is also very hard. You have to both look up and see the beauty and look down and do the work."

As you read stories of stewards throughout history, two essential characteristics begin to emerge: investment and transcendence. Put another way, stewards are those who fully invested in something bigger than themselves. At the Capurso Winery, you see these two essential building blocks of stewards on full display. For the Capurso family, the transcendent element is the beauty, and the investment aspect is the hard work. By keeping the two in balance, the Capursos have successfully operated their vineyard for more than 120 years.

Cincinnatus put his life and the lives of his family on the line—the ultimate investment—for the transcendent goal of preserving a Rome that served and represented all the people. Washington's transcendent cause was freedom and the right of self-governance, but it was far from free. It cost him eight years away from his beloved wife and his treasured residence at Mount Vernon. The servants in Jesus's parable invested all their efforts and energies for the higher purpose of producing a meaningful return for their master. And Horton, well, he worked and suffered to protect Whoville because, to him, "a person's a person, no matter how small." Each of these stewards made an enormous investment in something that was far bigger and far grander than himself.

Steward = Investment + Transcendence

## INVESTMENT

Imagine for a moment you were handed a first-place medal in the Ironman World Championship.[8] Held annually in Hawaii, the event combines a 2.4-mile rough water swim, followed by a 112-mile bike ride, topped off by a full marathon. Completing a grueling event like this is unthinkable for all but an elite group of athletes. So, here is the question: would you value that medal? Probably not. Would you wear it around your neck with pride? Almost certainly not. By contrast, a person who competes in the event and actually *wins* it might never want to take such a medal off. It would likely be one of his or her most prized possessions.

So, the real question is this: why would this medal mean so much to one person and so little to another? It's not the financial value of the medal itself. Rather, the answer is its cost. Over the course of nearly a quarter century of doing estate planning, one of the central lessons I have learned is this: we value things based on what they *cost* us—not just in money, but also in effort, risk, stress, sacrifice, and persistence. When something comes to us for nothing, we simply do not, and cannot, value it nearly as much as something that has a personal cost. This, I believe, is the reason the average American inheritance lasts only eighteen months. A lifetime of earning and sacrifice is consumed by the recipients in less than two years, primarily because it comes to them without any true cost.

In his book *Skin in the Game*, Nassim Nicholas Taleb argues that risk is an essential element for decision-making because it adds *cost* to the outcome of those decisions. Too often, individuals, businesses, and policymakers seek to make decisions that come with limited personal cost, whether financial or otherwise. As Taleb sees it, the phrase *skin in the game* "is often mistaken for one-sided incentives: the promise of a bonus will make someone work harder for you. . . . [But] people should also be penalized if something for which they are responsible goes wrong and hurts others: he or she who wants a share of the benefits needs to also share some of the risks."[9] To truly have skin in the game, a person must stand to benefit when things go well, but also stand to face harm when things go poorly.

In Taleb's view, cost brings several important elements to the table. First, cost and risk are critical to help you understand what you value. As he points out in *Skin*, "How much you truly 'believe' in something can be manifested only through what you are willing to risk for it."[10] You can say you value being physically in shape, but if you don't get up early and head to the gym or go out for a run, the reality is that you don't actually *value* fitness, at least not to the level that you are willing to pay a cost for it. Standing up for what you think is right in the face of harm or potential negative personal consequence, on the other hand, is a fairly good indicator of what you value. As Charles Dickens said, "The important thing is this: to be ready at any moment to sacrifice what you are for what you could become."[11]

Second, according to Taleb, cost brings focus and clarity to a situation. The general who leads his troops into battle has likely assessed the situation far more thoroughly than the one who sends orders to "Charge!" from far away. When *we* are the ones who will ultimately pay the price, especially if it's a dear one, we tend to focus more intently on the details than when someone else is footing the bill. We typically only attempt to take the hill we want to take when it is worth both the cost and the risk.

Third, cost forces us to constantly think and adapt. That's because cost is often associated with pain, loss, and struggle. When we face trials and difficulties, we are forced to change, modify our behavior, or double down and persevere. Why? Because we want the pain to end. Martin Luther King Jr. put it this way: "As my sufferings mounted, I soon realized that there were two ways that I could respond to my situation—either to react with bitterness or seek to transform the suffering into a creative force. I decided to follow the latter course."[12]

Finally, having skin in the game, and taking on both the benefits and the burdens of one's decisions, is ultimately an act of honor and courage. Taleb posits that when we set ourselves up to benefit from something that does not come with a personal cost—or worse, that comes at a potential cost to others—we are not acting honorably. Courage arises, or doesn't, in those moments in life when virtue meets cost. In Harper Lee's *To Kill a Mockingbird,* small-town lawyer Atticus Finch takes on the defense of a Black resident charged with a crime he didn't commit. Finch's willingness to mount the man's defense is a personally costly one, but is born of a belief that doing what is right makes the sacrifice worthwhile. Explaining to his daughter why he chose to mount a hopeless defense, Finch said this: "I wanted you to see what real courage is, instead of getting the idea that courage is a man with a gun in his hand. It's when you know you're licked before you begin, but you begin anyway, and you see it through no matter what."[13]

## Four Benefits of Cost

1. *Cost and risk are critical to help you understand what you value.*

2. *Cost brings focus and clarity to a situation.*

3. *Cost forces us to constantly think and adapt.*

4. *Taking on both the benefits and the burdens of one's decisions is ultimately an act of honor and courage.*

So, cost is what generates value. And there are three principal things a person can invest in that create personal and meaningful cost. These are the often-cited three *T*s: time, talent, and treasure.

### TIME

Time is unique among the three types of investment because it is the only one that is allocated equally (at least on a daily basis) to everyone. Because of this unique characteristic, time is also the investment that is typically the most valued. It is certainly the one that is most talked about. The Oxford English Corpus is the division of the Oxford Dictionaries tasked with building and growing a database of every single English word disseminated on the internet, whether in formal literature, blogs, social media posts, or news articles.[14] So, what noun tops all others when combing through the World Wide Web, with a hodgepodge of trillions of words? You guessed it—it's *time*.[15]

The value of time comes across clearly when we talk about it. We guard time, watch it, measure it, spend it, save it, relish it, march to it, share it, and—yes—waste it (which in itself is an acknowledgement of its value). Modern appliances are so essential to us not because they do things we couldn't do ourselves but because they *save* us time that we can then *spend* elsewhere. We use time to determine the worth of our various pursuits. We say things like, "That was well worth the time spent on it," and "That was a complete waste of my time."

One of the most unique and frustrating aspects of time is that even though it can be measured objectively, we perceive it differently as we age. The phrase "Oh, how the time flies," is actually based in reality. Scientists have observed for years that as people age, their perception of time accelerates, though there is no clear consensus on why. Some believe that time appears to speed up because humans perceive novel experiences in a more acute and "slowed-down" way than repeated experiences, and so as we age and develop habits and routines, our perception of time begins to quicken. Others think that as we age, each year represents a smaller relative chunk of our total lives. Thus, each passing year seems shorter than the last.

Adrian Bejan, a professor of mechanical engineering at Duke University, has a different take. He thinks the difference in our perception of time is based in neuroscience.[16] Bejan believes that because young brains are constantly creating new pathways, they work much more rapidly, and can take in far more information per second, than older brains. And so, counterintuitively, their perception of time is relatively slow. As we age, our brain develops many more established pathways for input to travel along, but some of those pathways become degraded over time. The reduced amount of information we can process per second actually speeds up our perception of the passage of time. Regardless of the actual reasons, the reality is that time becomes ever more valuable to us as we age, not only because we begin to appreciate its limited supply, but also because of the very way we perceive it.

In their book, *The Time Paradox: The New Psychology of Time That Will Change Your Life,* psychologists Philip Zimbardo and John Boyd give some practical suggestions about how we can slow down time, or at least our perception of it, as we age. First, invest in as many new, different, and unique experiences as possible. Repeated acts don't create new memories, and our brain essentially skips over them, like hitting the fast-forward button. Second, spend time focusing on positive experiences from your past and being more aware of your present. Third, focus on having a positive, optimistic, and hopeful perspective of your future. Your anticipation of future good will actually have the effect of you feeling as if the present is moving slower.

Time is not only precious in its own right, but it also brings value to anything connected to time, a fact that has not gone unnoticed in marketing. To prove this, Jennifer Aaker, a professor of marketing at the Stanford Graduate School of Business, conducted a rather simple experiment. Aaker and her team enlisted two six-year-olds and tasked them with running a lemonade stand. The kids used three different signs, at different times, to advertise their little operation. The first sign read, "Spend a little time and enjoy C&D's lemonade." The second read, "Spend a little money and enjoy C&D's lemonade." And the third read simply, "Enjoy C&D's lemonade." Not only did the sign that referenced time attract twice as many customers, but those customers were willing to pay twice as much for the lemonade.[17] Aaker's coauthor, Cassie Mogilner, expressed this idea about the value of time: "Ultimately, time is a more scarce resource—once it's gone, it's gone—and therefore more meaningful to us. How we spend our time says so much more about who we are than does how we spend our money."[18] Aaker and Mogiler note that marketers are so in tune with the value of time that nearly half of all advertisements make either a direct or indirect reference to time.

## TALENT

The second principal source of investment is talent, which comprises our personal skills, abilities, know-how, aptitudes, experiences, and personalities. Unlike time, the kinds of talents we possess are as numerous and diverse as the human race. As a result, talent allows for a greater range of individuality than the other types of investment when it comes to expression. Whereas time is a uniform constant for everyone, and treasure, which we'll discuss in a moment, is a finite, external resource, talent is both intimately personal and infinitely expressive. It is about how our inner world connects with the outer world and how the outer world views—and, for good or bad, often values—us as humans.

Although talent is as unique as each individual on the planet, it does entail one unifying constant that is found across every person deemed talented: work. As one author noted, "No one ever walks backwards into talent."[19] For talent to grow and develop, it must be nurtured in the soil of effort and time.

In his best-selling book *Outliers,* Malcolm Gladwell proffers what he calls the 10,000-hour rule, which refers to the general amount of time it takes for someone to fully develop a talent or ability. Gladwell came to this rule, and his conclusion that talent requires a significant investment of time and effort, based on the research and work of Anders Ericsson, a professor of psychology at Florida State University. Ericsson, along with Robert Pool, later authored *Peak: Secrets from the New Science of Expertise.* In their book, Ericsson and Pool take the position that Gladwell's rule and observations are not quite right.[20]

The *Peak* authors agree with Gladwell that excelling at a skill is a matter of practice rather than innate talent, and that people are better off applying themselves in an area they are interested in rather than trying to find their "true calling" based on their perceived natural abilities. That said, they note a couple of points that are important to understand about the so-called 10,000-hour rule.

First, there is nothing magical about that particular measure of time. Gladwell pulled that number from the average amount of time it took concert violinists to perfect their craft by age twenty. The actual number of hours for any specific person could be considerably greater or fewer, depending on the innate ability of the individual and particular skill being mastered. While effort does correlate with proficiency, each of us has natural abilities and proclivities that make certain tasks easier or harder for us. Second, and perhaps most importantly, mastery is not merely a product of the *amount* of time you spend, but also of *how* you spend that time. In other words, it's about quantity time *and* quality time. Ericsson and Pool use the term *deliberate practice* to describe a process that involves not only repetition but also "constantly pushing oneself beyond one's comfort zone, following training activities designed by an expert to develop specific abilities, and using feedback to identify weaknesses and work on them."[21]

## TREASURE

The third and final source of investment is treasure,[22] which consists of our money, physical resources, and tools. While commonly thought of first when we hear the word *investment*, treasure is actually the last in order of importance of the three types of investments and can potentially be the most deceptive because its reality differs so much from our common perception.

Typically seen as a *lead driver* of investment and return, treasure is actually much more often a *lagging indicator* of the combined effect of time and talent drawn together by effort. Although "It takes money to make money" and "The rich get richer, and the poor get poorer" are commonly accepted truisms in the world today, the reality is that treasure is far more often accumulated by those who earn it through an investment of time and talent than it is simply bestowed on people by fortune or family. Nearly half of the companies listed in the Fortune 500 in 2017 were founded either by immigrants who came to the United States with few resources or by the children of such immigrants—a fascinating statistic, considering the fact that immigrants represent only about 14 percent of the total population.[23] Another study found that more than one-third of the innovators in the United States were immigrants to this country and an additional 10 percent were the child of a first-generation immigrant. That means that nearly half of all innovation in the United States (defined by patents received and/

or innovation awards granted) was done by first or second-generation immigrants.[24] In 2018, two-thirds of the Forbes 400 Richest Americans were self-made individuals who started with little to no wealth themselves.

While access to at least some level of capital is usually necessary to start, build, or grow a business enterprise, treasure typically follows other types of investment and is not the true creator of treasure itself. Gail Miller, the Utah Jazz "owner" we met in the introduction, was so poor growing up that she remembers having to move the family's single lightbulb from the kitchen to the living room after dinner because they could not afford bulbs in every room. When she and her husband, Larry, were married, they had only high school educations and worked blue-collar jobs just to make ends meet.

While some may say that treasure that comes from inheritance is an exception to the rule that treasure follows investment, in actuality, it's a type of treasure that typically doesn't last precisely because of the lack of personal cost—despite the posits of some prominent authors. Thomas Piketty, for example, in 2014's *Capital in the Twenty-First Century*, detailed his concerns about the issues of concentration of wealth, income inequality, and the distribution of capital, as well as the likely effects of those forces in the future. Based on the premise that invested capital always grows at a rate faster than general macroeconomic growth, Piketty posited that wealthy individuals and families grow their wealth disproportionately faster than the general population, and therefore, that income inequality and its many perceived issues will only accelerate in the future. His book, a *New York Times* bestseller, has been cited by many as a reason for using tax policies and other measures to reduce or eliminate the concentration of wealth among the few.

Researchers Robert Arnott, William Bernstein, and Lillian Wu, however, took a deep dive into Piketty's work and came to the opposite conclusion. They found that wealth, or treasure, in America doesn't actually endure along generational lines, especially if it's not worked and reinvested. Among their findings, "The average wealth erosion for the ten wealthiest families of 1930, 1957, and 1968 . . . was 6.6 percent, 5.3 percent, and 8.7 percent, respectively. These figures correspond to a half-life of wealth—the length of time it takes for half of the family fortune to be redistributed within society through taxation, spending, and charitable giving—of ten years, thirteen years, and (remarkably) eight years, respectively."[25] Assuming, for example, a half-life of eight years, that would mean that a person who inherits $20 million would have $2.5 million left after just twenty-four years, or just one generation. (Perhaps the familiar saying about fools and money should be adapted to "An *heir* and his money are soon parted.")

We must also consider the idea that the same amount of treasure isn't always valued equally by everyone. As noted earlier in the chapter, a critical component of value is cost. When treasure is earned from effort, persistence, or creativity, it carries a weight and worth that unearned resources simply cannot carry. This "relative value" aspect of financial resources even applies to earned versus borrowed money. It's long been known by psychologists (and marketing experts) that we tend to spend more when we use credit cards than when we use cash. That's because parting with cash triggers the pain receptors in our brains, whereas credit card use does not. According to researchers, the pleasure of receiving the goods or services coupled with the pain of losing the cash serves as a natural deterrent to overspending. When we *de*couple the pleasure and the pain, and defer the pain until the Visa bill arrives, we tend to spend more because the pain isn't present to act as a moderating force.

While it's easy to intuitively understand the connection between using cash and spending less, what may be surprising to learn is that the *way* we pay for something carries over to our perception of the value of the item purchased. In a series of experiments conducted by Avni Shah and her colleagues, published in *The Journal of Consumer Research*,[26] Shah discovered that the more pain we associate with the cost of an item, the more we value that item. In one experiment, the researchers sold students mugs with a value of $7 for $2 each. Half of the students paid with credit cards; the other half paid in cash.

The researchers later announced they had sold the mugs by mistake and needed to buy them back. Because the "mistake" had been made through no fault of the student, the students were allowed to set a fair price for selling their new mugs back.

Those who purchased the mugs with credit cards were generally willing to sell them back at an average price of $3.83. Those who paid with cash, however, were more reluctant to sell the mugs back and also demanded a higher price—on average, $6.71, or nearly double the amount of their plastic-paying compatriots. In other words, those who experienced even the small amount of pain associated with having to hand over $2 from their own pocket ended up valuing their purchase twice as much as the people who hadn't experienced that same pain. In a second experiment, students were asked to donate $5 to a given charity, with half making the donation in cash and the other half via a voucher they were provided at no cost. In both cases, students were given a pin they could wear to memorialize their support. Those who paid with cash were more than three times more likely to wear their pins (51 percent) than those who provided support through a free voucher (14 percent).

The bottom line is this: investment—as evidenced through pain and cost—brings a value and clarity to financial decision-making that is difficult to replicate when that key building block is absent. This connection between pain and value is so powerful that several high-end brands are considering making purchasing their products *more difficult* by requiring customers to pay with cash or take other additional steps so that they associate that additional cost (and thus value) to their brand.[27]

## TRANSCENDENCE

Transcendence is the second building block of stewardship. Transcendence is a word on the rise in the modern lexicon. Since 1940, its use in English literature has increased more than threefold. The word is derived from the Latin *transcendentem,* which literally means "to rise above" and refers to that which lies beyond, and is greater than, oneself or one's circumstances. People who have overcome challenging life situations are said to have transcended their circumstances.

The quintessential example of transcendence is, of course, the concept of God, whether we adopt the traditional view of God found in various world religions or a more general view of God as a form of universal intelligence.[28] Transcendence can also be found in our highest and noblest values, ideals, and virtues. Whether we find transcendence in the Judeo-Christian version of God or in a belief in qualities such as justice, compassion, beauty, and honor, there are certain common characteristics that transcendent things share.

## IT'S A BIG DEAL

First and foremost, transcendence entails a connection to something bigger than us, and usually, the bigger, the better. Transcendence occurs when a new and grander perspective beyond us comes into play.

Manned flight—whether through air travel or space travel—is a relatively recent phenomenon in human history, beginning in earnest in just the last century. Prior to this development, humans' perspective on life had been, well, fairly grounded. In 1987, however, Frank White coined the term *overview effect* to describe the sensation astronauts experience when they see Earth from above for the first time.[29] Borders disappear, and the beauty, mystery, and connectedness of our tiny blue orb floating in the vastness of empty space becomes real, felt, and experienced. Michael Collins, a member of the Apollo 11 crew with Neil Armstrong and Buzz Aldrin, describes it this way: "The thing that really surprised me was that it [Earth] projected an air of fragility. And why, I don't know. I don't know to this day. I had a feeling it's tiny, it's shiny, it's beautiful, it's home, and it's fragile."[30] This effect has not been limited to American astronauts. Yuri Gagarin, the first person to venture into space, was a cosmonaut who expressed the same feelings (translated from Russian to English): "Orbiting Earth in the spaceship, I saw how beautiful our planet is. People, let us preserve and increase this beauty, not destroy it!"[31]

More recent space explorers have echoed similar themes. In May 2020, the United States, through SpaceX, resumed launching humans into space for the first time since the end of the space shuttle program nine years prior. First-time astronaut Bob Behnken described his perspective from space this way: "You see that it's a single planet with a shared atmosphere. It's our shared place in this universe. So I think that perspective, as we go through things like the pandemic or we see the challenges across our nation or across the world, [makes us] recognize that we all face them together."[32] Astronaut Kathryn D. Sullivan said, "I'm happy to report that no amount of prior study or training can fully prepare anybody for the awe and wonder this inspires."[33]

The overview effect, like many other experiences of transcendence, creates a paradoxical response: it makes us feel incredibly small while also imparting a sense of peace and joy that comes from a deep connection to everyone and everything around us. The immensity of something that is so much bigger than us also makes us feel *more important,* in a strange way, because of our connection to that bigger thing. That is why engaging with something bigger than ourselves is so vitally important.

The overview effect is, in many ways, the opposite of psychosis, which is the state of losing touch with reality. A psychotic episode happens when someone becomes detached from the reality of their surroundings. All they can sense is their inner processes, and they lose connection with what is actually going on around them. The overview effect and other transcendent experiences, on the other hand, are expansive rather than reductive. They bring us a fuller picture of where we live, who we are, and how connected we are to everyone else.

## IT'S ABOUT OTHERS

Second, transcendence connects us to morality and to other people. Not only is transcendence about something bigger than us, but it also possesses an others-centered quality. Abraham Maslow is generally recognized as one of the top psychologists of the twentieth century and was the architect of the oft-cited Maslow's hierarchy of needs. When we think about his pyramid of needs, we usually place "self-actualization," or fulfilling one's individual potential, at the top. Maslow, however, saw something even greater as the pinnacle: self-transcendence—not merely freedom *for* yourself, but freedom *from* yourself. Maslow said it this way: "Transcendence refers to the very highest and most inclusive or holistic levels of human consciousness, behaving and relating, as ends rather than means, to oneself, to significant others, to human beings in general, to other species, to nature, and to the cosmos."[34] For Maslow, transcendence engenders what he called "peak experiences," which occur when an individual rises above their own personal needs, wants, or concerns and sees beyond, to others and to the ideal. These peak experiences lead to positive emotions like peace, joy, and expanded awareness.

Maslow is certainly not the only expert to recognize the importance of transcendence to emotional and mental well-being. Viktor Frankl was a twentieth-century psychiatrist and survivor of four separate Nazi concentration camps. In 1946, over a nine-day period, he wrote *Man's Search for Meaning,* which in 1991 was named as one of the ten most influential books in the United States by the Library of Congress. In his book, Frankl described the potential problems of a virtue such as freedom when it is not tethered to caring for others: "Freedom is not the last word. Freedom is only part of the story and half of the truth. Freedom is but the negative aspect of the whole phenomenon whose positive aspect is responsibleness. In fact, freedom is in danger of degenerating into mere arbitrariness unless it is lived in terms of responsibleness."[35]

Frankl realized that freedom unmoored to a sense of others is simply self-absorption masquerading as virtue. In fact, he thought so highly of linking others-centeredness to freedom that he championed the idea of a "Statue of Responsibility" to be built on the West Coast to complement the Statue of Liberty on the East Coast. For Frankl, transcendent meaning in human life is inextricably tied to our sense of responsibility to one another.

## IT INSPIRES AWE

Finally, for something to be truly transcendent, it must create at least some level of awe. Awe is defined (by Merriam-Webster) as "an emotion variously combining dread, veneration, and wonder that is inspired by authority or by the sacred or sublime." It causes us to stop what we are doing and drop our jaws in response. Like the overview effect, awe has the power to pull us out of ourselves and make us experience something that is external, powerful, and transformative. Awe is difficult to describe by those who experience it because it elicits such a wide variety of feelings and emotions. By its nature, it takes us beyond what we can normally process or understand.

Because awe is such a powerful force, it has become the focus of its own study and research. The Lab of Misfits is a collection of some of the most diverse experts you will find in any endeavor. It consists of neuroscientists, artists, designers, and business experts, who research topics as varied as their backgrounds. To study the concept of awe, the Lab teamed up with Cirque du Soleil in Las Vegas, Nevada. Known for its mesmerizing, death-defying shows, Cirque seemed like the perfect venue for studying the effects of awe on the human psyche.[36] To do its study, the Lab ran two different experiments on a group of 282 audience members. For the first experiment, the researchers hooked up sixty of the subjects to EEG monitors to record real-time data on how the brains of the audience members perceived the unfolding events of the Cirque show *O*. The brain activity of the participants was tracked throughout the show to see whether and how it changed during certain particularly awe-inspiring moments.

One of the most fascinating results from this test was that when participants experienced moments of awe, their prefrontal cortex, which is the part of the brain that acts as our decision-maker, decreased in activity while the part of the brain that manages creativity and memory increased in activity. The subjects' brains began to think less about the self and began to open up to what was going on around them in a broader and more communal sense.

For the second experiment, the Lab surveyed the audience members just after they finished watching the show. Researchers used a version of the identification with all humanity (IWAH) scale, a standard diagnostic test that helps psychologists determine how connected an individual feels to their community and the world around them.[37] People with higher IWAH scores tend to feel deeper connections with humanity as a whole and tend to have a more positive, altruistic perspective toward others. The participants also took an electronic version of the Balloon Analogue Risk Task, which is a measure of risk tolerance, as well as other psychological tests.

Those audience members who reported feeling awe during the show scored significantly higher on IWAH questions related to their perceived connection to humanity as a whole. The awe created by the show actually created an environment in which the participants felt like they were part of something bigger than themselves.

Combining the results from all this testing, the Lab came to several conclusions. According to Cirque du Soleil's own summary of the study, the experience of awe does the following:

1.  Leads to fully living in the moment. This finding suggests that in a state of awe, we draw our focus away from our never-ending thoughts and distractions and into the sights and sounds around us. Somehow awe packs enough disruptive punch for us to immerse ourselves into an experience.

2.  Enhances our willingness to step into the unknown, including an openness and a disposition to ask questions, lean into new experiences, and be more empathetic toward others.

3.  Increases our tolerance to risk, creating a lower need for cognitive control, a decreased need to "be right," and the ability to accept information in a less biased manner. This ultimately contributes to an increased curiosity and overall desire to step into the unknown.

4.  Recalibrates our feelings about the future and reshapes our perceptions about the past. Perhaps the most striking discovery, this reframing of one's positive sense of self may magnify the behavioral effects of an awe experience and suggests a mechanism for more persistent behavioral change. This reinforces the hypothesis that awe may one day be used to foster psychological wellness.

5.  Puts the brain in a state of bliss, counteracting the effect of stress and reflecting neural characteristics associated with those induced by psychedelics.

6.  Can lead to increased creativity due to a greater activity in the default-mode network, a brain function most commonly associated with self-related thinking, such as meditation, which plays a large role when reflecting on the self or others.[38]

Awe, of course, is not limited to the bright lights of a Vegas stage; it can be experienced at the base of a majestic mountain, savored in the depths of a massive canyon, and felt viscerally when holding a newborn child. Regardless of the triggering mechanism, awe empowers us to take in the world beyond ourselves in new ways, which results in our feeling more engaged, alive, and connected to others.

•  •  •

So, we have looked at what a steward is, and we have examined the two fundamental building blocks of stewardship: investment and transcendence. In the next chapter, we will strengthen our understanding of stewardship by looking at certain character types in which one or more of these two essential building blocks is absent.

# CHAPTER 2

# Consumers, Dreamers, and Owners

*"You wanna fly, you got to give up the . . .*
*[stuff] that weighs you down."*

**—Toni Morrison**

The world we live in is full of diversity, complexity, and change. It can be difficult to comprehend, much less navigate. Because of this, we often take one of two extreme approaches when trying to understand ourselves and our environments.

The first approach is to oversimplify. We try to make the complex simple. One common way we do this is by isolating just two factors from among a complexity of variables and then drawing conclusions based on how those two factors interact. For example, did you know that consuming more chocolate increases your chances of winning a Nobel Prize? That was the (facetious) finding of Dr. Franz Messerli in a paper he published in 2012 in *The New England Journal of Medicine*. Messerli's research found that countries with higher chocolate consumption tend to produce more Nobel Prize winners than countries with lower chocolate consumption.

The paper was actually a chocolate-covered, tongue-in-cheek attempt to point out the fallacy of conflating *causation* with *correlation.* Messerli's "research finding" deliberately missed the key variable: wealth. Wealthier nations not only focus more resources on science than poorer countries do—increasing the likelihood that Nobel Prize–worthy work will occur within their borders—they also happen to buy more of the sweet stuff because they can afford the luxury. Chocolate has no direct bearing on prize-winning science (at least that we know of). In his book *Spurious Correlations*, Tyler Vigen points out the problems associated with linking correlation to causation and gives some great examples of this fallacy in action.

On the other extreme, humans also tend to make simple things complicated. In our lives, our jobs, and our finances, we often add so many details and considerations to our attempted understanding of an issue that we can become frozen into indecision. Adding complexity to the simple has even become a competitive art form of sorts. American inventor and cartoonist Reuben Goldberg became famous for his drawings of outlandishly complex gadgets designed to do simple tasks. His cartoons gave rise not only to the term "Rube Goldberg machine" but also to national and international competitions. The current record for the most complex Rube Goldberg machine was accomplished by a Purdue University team that built a 300-step machine for the sole purpose of blowing up and popping a balloon.

As explained in the previous chapter, the formula of stewardship is *investment plus transcendence equals steward.* Focusing on these two elements alone would indeed be an oversimplification; there are more aspects to stewardship than just investment and transcendence, not the least of which is the unique way stewards think—which we'll explore in a later chapter. However, these two building blocks do afford us a clear and useful way to conceptualize the idea of what makes someone a steward.

With that in mind, what does it look like when one or both of these critical elements—investment and transcendence—are missing? Let's examine three common character types to answer that question.

## CONSUMERS

A consumer is someone who invests little to nothing *and* sees no transcendent purpose in what they do. Essentially, consumers are the opposite of stewards. Consumers have a self-oriented focus, and they tend to have no real lasting impact on their corner of the world. Driven by expectation (of their needs being fulfilled), their perspective is one of entitlement—which is the habit of focusing on personal rights and privileges without factoring in any commensurate duties or obligation to others. Consumers tend to live with their heads down as they are guided by the concerns of the present and weighed down by what they possess, without realizing that often those possessions actually own them. They fail to look up to anything bigger than themselves or to look toward what they could accomplish.

## FOUR POSSIBLE DESTINATIONS

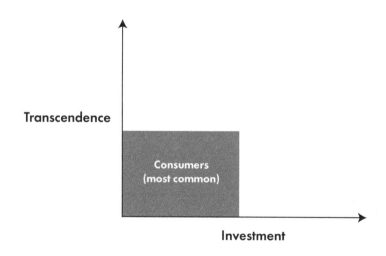

While we all live in a consumer culture and play the role of consumer to some extent every day, a consumer, as a character type, is someone who has a specific attitude and perspective on life that impacts how they engage with the world around them. The consumer mentality is all too common when it comes to inheritance. This may be attributable, in large part, to the nature of traditional estate planning, which focuses almost exclusively on who is receiving the bequest. The traditional model transfers unearned wealth to heirs, with no cost, no meaning, and no purpose attached to the inheritance—and then we wonder why the wealth is consumed so quickly.

One of the most important facts to understand about consumerism is that it rarely, if ever, results in long-term happiness. "Money cannot buy happiness" is more than a casual aphorism. It carries with it an abiding truth, and *hedonic adaptation* is one of the main reasons it is true.

Hedonic adaptation is the idea that while positive and negative experiences *can* have an impact on our perceived level of happiness in the short term, our natural human tendency is to adjust to the change fairly quickly and to return to our prior level of happiness. Studies have shown, for example, that the happiness level of lottery winners a year after their win is the same as, or lower than, it was prior to their win. The opposite is also true. A separate study found that although people who become paralyzed after an accident experience a dramatic decrease in their perceived level of happiness, they generally return to their pre-accident levels of happiness once they get used to their new life situation.

A persistent notion also exists among consumers that their lack of happiness stems from the fact that they don't have enough money and possessions—and that once they acquire more stuff, then they will be content and happy. Those who have actually acquired substantial stuff, however, beg to differ. According to a 2018 survey of the very wealthiest Americans, conducted by US Trust, only about half of the respondents were very satisfied with how they spend their money (53 percent), fewer than half were very satisfied with how they spend their *time* (43 percent), only 19 percent said that more money would make life better, and only 4 percent thought more stuff would make life better.

This experience is no less true among those with more modest means, especially when it comes to homes and possessions. Larger homes have certainly been the trend in the United States, where the average home size has increased from 1,500 square feet in 1973 to nearly 2,500 square feet in 2015. At the same time, *family size* has actually gone down—so new homes now offer an average of 971 square feet per person, up from roughly 500 square feet in the 1970s.[39] While home space has nearly doubled, overall satisfaction with our homes has stayed about the same. As we have adjusted to bigger homes with more bathrooms and amenities, our "home happiness" level has not increased. In fact, satisfaction with our big residences can actually go down if someone else builds a bigger home near ours. Social comparison is a major happiness killer.

Consumers have also been on an acquisition frenzy since the end of WWII, with a resulting frenzy of material acquisitions that can't fit in those ever-larger homes. Self-storage facilities have now become a $100 billion industry[40]—we have more stuff than we can fit in our homes—and yet the prevalence of major depression has increased tenfold since 1945.[41]

All this said, there *is* a correlation between resources and happiness, but only to a point. The first bite of cheesecake may be heavenly—the twelfth, not so much. Just because *some* of a thing is good, it doesn't mean more is better. In a massive analysis by the Department of Psychological Sciences at Purdue University that was published in the journal *Nature Human Behaviour*,[42] which used data from the Gallup World Poll from more than 1.7 million people across 164 countries, researchers learned several interesting things about the correlation between money and happiness. To no one's great surprise, they did find a correlation between income level and happiness. For example, if someone made $40,000 and their income was increased to $50,000, their perceived level of happiness also increased. But once a person reached a certain level of income, their happiness level stopped rising.

In the United States, depending on the area of the country and the relative cost of living, that ideal income level for happiness tends to be reached between $60,000 and $75,000 a year. While that may be the sweet spot for feeling positive emotions on a day-to-day basis, the researchers found that a higher figure—$95,000—is ideal for "life evaluation," which takes into account long-term goals, peer comparisons, and other macro-level metrics. What came as a surprise to the researchers from Purdue was that it may be possible to make too much money, at least as far as happiness is concerned. They observed *declines* in emotional well-being and life satisfaction after the $95,000 mark.

The researchers came up with three reasons for this counterintuitive drop. First, earning greater amounts of money is typically associated with additional work and stress. Second, as people make more money, they begin to compare themselves more to others, and this social comparison leads to increased dissatisfaction (just as it does with larger homes). The third reason, though, is perhaps the most interesting. Researchers determined that at a $95,000-a-year income level in the United States, you can, for the most part, get everything you need to live, and so the excess income allows you to switch from needs to wants.

Needs can be quantified—but wants can be insatiable. There is always a faster car, a bigger boat, a better vacation, and the inability to acquire more of those things can actually result in our being less happy than we were when our focus was mainly on everyday needs and concerns.

As mentioned earlier, consumers, as a character type, lack both meaningful investment and transcendent purpose. The absence of these critical components means that consumers tend to be rather disengaged from the world around them. Too often they have a self-focused mentality, which makes their lives feel compact, chaotic, and overwhelming. Because they tend to look down at their feet below them and not upward and outward at the horizon in front of them, consumers can easily feel jostled and tossed about, myopic, alienated. They lack the sense of purpose that comes from connecting to something bigger than themselves and the value that comes from investing at a personal cost, leaving consumers trapped within a self-imposed prison of stuff.

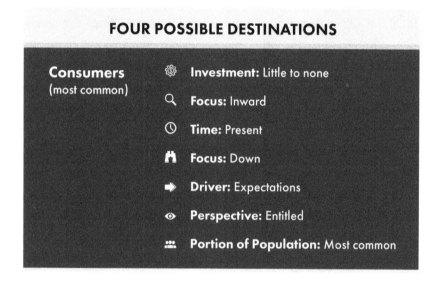

## DREAMERS

A dreamer is someone who is driven by a transcendent purpose but either lacks the ability to invest his or her time, talent, and treasure or chooses not to make such a personal investment (or, perhaps most tragically, simply has never been asked to invest). Unlike consumers, dreamers are not self-absorbed. Rather, their focus is outward, they are driven by meaning, and their perspective is an enriching one. They truly want to see positive change and a better, brighter tomorrow. Dreamers tend to be creative, imaginative, and curious. They are constantly thinking about how things could, or should, be ideally different. Unlike consumers who live with their heads down, dreamers live with their heads up and can literally even exist with their "heads in the clouds." While they may not be focused primarily on themselves and their possessions, they nevertheless fail to have forward motion and, as a result, end up just as mired in place as consumers.

## FOUR POSSIBLE DESTINATIONS

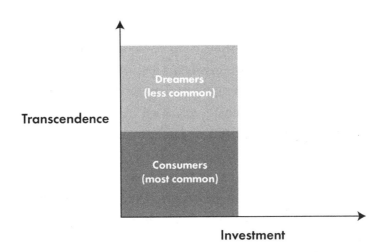

For many dreamers, the problem isn't one of caring too much, but rather one of caring *about* too much. Dreamers can become victims of their own imaginations and can be overwhelmed by all the things they want to do to make a difference. This can result in "dreamer-overload," a form of paralysis—when someone cares about everything, they often end up being unable to care for anything.

While dreamers can be an inspiration to others, they can also become fairly easily discouraged when others don't share their vision or don't believe in the dreamer's ability to effectuate change. The outward focus of dreamers can end up working against them, as they become too reliant on the opinions and perspectives of others. Lacking deep personal investment (or skin in the game, as Taleb would call it), they also tend to give up readily because their failure to follow through comes with little to no personal pain or loss.

Perhaps the biggest issue with dreamers is that they often combine a strong desire for the ideal with a lack of personal belief in themselves and their abilities. Tending toward perfectionism, dreamers can become their own worst enemies because of their capacity to think big of the world and little of themselves. Their perceived lack of competence in the face of their noble quests for perfection often leads to stress, procrastination, and inaction. Countless studies have shown a correlation between perfectionism and procrastination. That is because, owing to their overly high expectations, perfectionists see only potential failure in future endeavors and find avoiding situations a more attractive alternative than failing to achieve their desired outcome. Procrastination often results in increased anxiety, which then feeds the feelings of perceived failure and leads to further procrastination.

This curse of perfectionism may be getting worse. Researchers from the University of Bath and York St. John University studied the test results of more than 40,000 students who took the multidimensional perfectionism scale test over a three-decade period. The MPS measures three types of perfectionism: *self-oriented* (an irrational desire to be perfect), *socially prescribed* (the perception of excessive expectations from others), and *other-oriented* (the placing of unrealistic standards on others). The researchers found all three forms of perfectionism to be on the rise, with the self-oriented perfectionism score up by 10 percent from 1989 to 2016, the socially prescribed score up 33 percent, and the other-oriented score up by 16 percent.[43] Beyond simply triggering added stress, anxiety, and procrastination in younger people, perfectionism has also been correlated with suicide. Canadian researchers who interviewed friends and family of suicide victims found that a majority of those who took their lives were described as highly self-demanding.[44]

Finally, many dreamers who yearn to make a difference are ultimately dissuaded because they come to believe that what they want to accomplish will be monumentally difficult or impossible to achieve. In some cases, this belief is well founded. A little more than a month before his assassination, Martin Luther King Jr. gave what might be considered a prophetic sermon, titled, "Unfulfilled Dreams." Unlike his better-known "I Have a Dream" speech from five years earlier, this one carried a solemn, somber tone. Beginning with the biblical story of David, who strongly desired to build God a temple but was prevented from doing so, King described the fate of those who dream big dreams but fail to see them realized. He recounted the stories of Schubert's Unfinished Symphony, Mahatma Gandhi's inability to unite India and Pakistan, Woodrow Wilson's failed attempt at creating a League of Nations, and the apostle Paul's failure to personally deliver his message in Spain.

For all of these famous individuals, their dreams were bigger than their abilities, or at least bigger than their times. The question King attempted to address that day wasn't whether or not we should have a dream, but rather what to do when we "find ourselves . . . having to face the fact that our dreams are not fulfilled."[45] Ultimately, King came to see our dreams not as a final destination but rather as an endless road for us to travel. Dreams, according to King, are meant to provide us with both a guiding direction and an anchor to keep us from drifting away when buffeted by life's storms. In our internal and external battles of good and evil, our dreams help us to hold course and stay afloat, whether or not those dreams are ever actually realized. In King's words,

> Oh, this morning, if I can leave anything with you, let me urge you to be sure that you have a strong boat of faith. The winds are going to blow. The storms of disappointment are coming. The agonies and the anguishes of life are coming. And be sure that your boat is strong, and also be very sure that you have an anchor. In times like these, you need an anchor. And be very sure that your anchor holds.

Dreamers can often find themselves caught in an endless and fruitless loop of dreams they think (or even know) are dauntingly difficult to accomplish, crippling concerns over how they are perceived by others, and an inability to invest themselves in projects because of their paralyzing fear of failure. To escape this loop, dreamers should consider taking one or more of the following steps:

1.  Focus on becoming really good at something—anything— and then put that ability into practice. Completing a task through a newly developed skill set may help you overcome procrastination and may lead to engagement—which could eventually turn into engagement with your dreams (thus making you a steward). For many dreamers, the issue is a lack of confidence, and confidence is built only through practice and engagement. Success can become a virtuous cycle, an expanding upward spiral, especially for those with big dreams and lofty visions. According to Walt Disney, the secret of making dreams come true "can be summarized in four Cs. They are curiosity, confidence, courage, and constancy; and the greatest of all is confidence."[46]

2.  Make a short list of realistic things you want to see change. Focus your energies on small, measurable ways to implement your lofty desires. Before attempting to change the entire education system of the United States, consider ways you could make a difference in the elementary school across the street. Seek justice in your neighborhood or town before seeking it in the farthest reaches of the world. Achieving meaningful and impactful change, even in small ways, can be a powerful way to transform from dreamer to steward.

3.  Surround yourself with others who are willing to share their stories of trial and adversity, not just their stories of success and accomplishment. Rarely, if ever, is the road to

accomplishment a straightforward and smoothly paved path. It usually features many bumps, bruises, failures, and embarrassments along the way. We often imagine that people who achieve meaningful goals are simply lucky or blessed by fate. Hearing true stories of what they really went through to move the needle can help a dreamer understand that perfection is an ideal that does not exist in reality.

4. If you are a dreamer, be willing to settle for "good enough" whenever reasonably possible, especially if you have perfectionistic tendencies and feel the need for every possibility to be maximized to the fullest. Psychologist Barry Schwartz and his team call this technique "satisficing," which essentially means being willing to accept a strategy and outcome that is sufficient to the demands of the situation without being driven to seek the best possible option. In other words, go with whatever works. Doing certain tasks at a "good" level is often far more productive than trying to do everything at the very highest level.

## FOUR POSSIBLE DESTINATIONS

**Dreamers**
(less common)

- **Investment:** Unable or unwilling to invest
- **Focus:** Outward
- **Time:** Future
- **Focus:** Up
- **Driver:** Meaning
- **Perspective:** Enriching
- **Portion of Population:** Less common

## OWNERS

In contrast to a dreamer, an owner is someone who maximizes their productivity, implements their talent, and invests their treasure. Owners are all in, all the time. They have an inward drive, they see the present with clear eyes, they know what is needed right now, and they know how to meet that need. They are motivated by ROI (return on investment), and their perspective is an enterprising one. Unlike consumers and dreamers who struggle with movement, owners are all about pushing forward. With a ready-fire-aim mentality, they are the builders, creators, and sustainers of community and culture. They are the first ones at the office, school, church, or kitchen table, and the last to leave. The issue for owners is that, while they have a forward focus on the road ahead, they too often fail to look up and see the grander, bigger picture. Their productivity and drive also results in the accumulation of lots of possessions, which, like with consumers, can sometimes result in holding them down.

## FOUR POSSIBLE DESTINATIONS

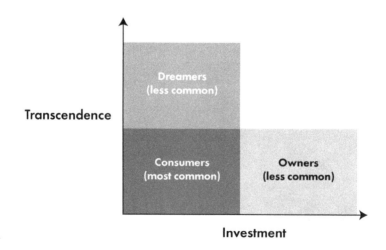

The owner mentality is not limited to business. It is a perspective that drives the parent who pours their heart and soul into their children, the employee who works to the breaking point to make a mark at work, and the student who tirelessly strives for the A because it looks so good on paper (or electronic screen). Owners are the first to step up and invest, volunteer, and serve. If you want to get something done, talk to an owner.

Over the years, I have been fortunate to work with many successful entrepreneurs, who are perhaps the quintessential examples of owners. One day, I decided to start asking them the "secret" to their success. I wanted to find out what principles and actions they embraced to start, run, and grow vibrant businesses. I quickly learned there were more differences to their approaches than similarities. Some said they were successful because they went it alone, called the shots, and made sure the buck stopped with them. Others said they were successful only because of their partners or team members. Some avoided debt like the plague while others used (and used and used) every bit of credit they could get their hands on to leverage their operations. Some sought outside investors while others bootstrapped their entire operations.

I finally did find one common characteristic of successful entrepreneurs, however: they could clearly see the myriad risks in front of them, and they accepted them. Conversely, I have seen countless failed businessmen and businesswomen who refused to acknowledge the risks and saw only the potential upside. Because they could not see the storms coming, they were completely unprepared for them when they struck. I have also seen those who were fearful to venture forth on their own because the risks of waves kept them perennially stuck on the shoreline, looking out at whatever potential trouble might lie just beyond the horizon.

Successful entrepreneurs are the ones who see all the risks, look them in the eye, and step into the ring regardless. It's not arrogance or hubris that pushes them forward; it is belief in themselves and their abilities in spite of the obstacles they face.

Although owners are fully engaged and invested, the missing element for them, when compared with stewards, is transcendence. For owners, their business, family, or organization, and what they produce within that construct, becomes their stand-in for transcendence. Many owners fail to realize that profit, production, and prestige can never be a lasting replacement for purpose. Daily, monthly, and quarterly goals can become a drug, not a dream, keeping owners in a perennial state of longing for their next "hit" from their financial statement, the attendance figures of their last event, or their child's most recent report card.

When the business, job, family, or position lacks a greater purpose, it can actually ensnare the owner and their ego without their even knowing it. They end up being owned by the results of their labor, not the other way around. They become trapped inside their accomplishments, lost and purposeless without them.

The lack of a transcendent purpose becomes a glaring problem when the object of the owner's focus comes to an end, as it inevitably does. For business owners, that often happens when they sell their business. Instead of rejoicing in the financial fruits of their labor, many business owners find themselves feeling lost and rudderless after a sale. Such was the case for James Averdieck, who turned his small chocolate pudding business, Gü, into an eight-figure payday. Instead of bringing Averdieck a sense of peace and accomplishment, the sale left him depressed and struggling. This experience is so common it even has a name: post-sale blues. A 2013 survey conducted by PricewaterhouseCoopers found that a full 75 percent of business owners regretted selling their business within just one year of the sale.

Businesspeople are not the only owners who experience these struggles and difficulties. Many stay-at-home parents, for example, are highly invested in the lives, activities, and education of their children. When the kids finally move onward and upward, the formerly fully engaged parent can end up experiencing many of the same issues and emotions of an entrepreneur after a business sale. So-called empty-nest syndrome can include many of the same "symptoms" as post-sale blues: depression, identity crisis, substance abuse, and relational issues. The children served as the "transcendent" reason for the parents' high-level investment, and when the kids are gone, so is the purpose for the investment. As a result, many parents who were highly involved in their children's lives have trouble finding meaning, direction, and engagement when the once-noisy house goes silent. The freedom that seemed so enticing during the days of chasing the toddler or driving the carpool now feels like a void. The rudder that guided so much of their lives is now missing.

When one draws one's purpose, meaning, and drive from a temporary source, a "day of reckoning" eventually arrives. The business is sold, the career comes to an end, the child moves out, the physical prowess or beauty of youth fades. When the thing the owner has focused all their investment in comes to the end of its clock, the owner is left without their *why.*

A more fulfilling way to live is to focus on timeless, high-level values like excellence, justice, and equality and to continually try to express those values through work or family. Failing to do this, owners unwittingly set course for a finite, limited purpose they will ultimately outlast. Their work at the office or in the home, rather than serving as an engaged expression of their higher values, becomes an end in itself. Their *role* becomes their identity. They fail to achieve the inner peace that comes from pursuing a transcendent ideal that creates direction and drive but offers no final destination.

Compassion and justice are not things we can check off our list; they're never finished. And so, pursuing such inspiring but unreachable aspirations paradoxically allows us to slow down and enjoy the journey toward what can never be fully achieved, as opposed to pressing relentlessly toward a discrete finish line, which, though attainable, ultimately offers an unsatisfying reward. In a life spent with no finite endgame, the expression of our essential values along the road, however long, becomes itself the endgame.

Another potential issue for owners, especially those who are entrepreneurs, is that they tend to have exaggerated personalities and lack balance in their lives, factors that can be exacerbated by their lack of transcendence. Though they're able to use the strengths of their unique personalities to set them apart in business, that asymmetry often comes at great cost. According to one study that compared entrepreneurs with the general population,[47] entrepreneurs were found to be twice as likely to suffer from depression, six times more likely to have ADHD, three times more likely to deal with substance abuse, and a staggering eleven times more likely to be bipolar than the general population as a whole. While certainly worthy of a chicken-and-egg analysis (i.e., did entrepreneurism *cause* these issues, or does the presence of these tendencies steer a person toward entrepreneurism as an outlet or coping mechanism), the reality is that entrepreneurs face many issues and struggles beyond merely creating and sustaining a business. Even entrepreneurs who say they don't have any diagnosable mental challenges are twice as likely as non-entrepreneurs to come from families with mental issues. A high level of investment, while a powerful tool for accomplishing goals, can mask underlying issues that need to be addressed.

## FOUR POSSIBLE DESTINATIONS

| | |
|---|---|
| **Owners** (less common) | ⚙ **Investment:** Deeply invested |
| | 🔍 **Focus:** Inward |
| | 🕐 **Time:** Present |
| | ♜ **Focus:** Forward |
| | ➡ **Driver:** Return |
| | 👁 **Perspective:** Enterprising |
| | 👥 **Portion of Population:** Less common |

## SITUATIONS AND SEASONS

I love Demotivators®—a series of posters from the brilliant people at despair.com, which take satirical spins on the motivational posters that were ubiquitous in the 1980s and 1990s. One of my favorites is a close-up picture of snowflakes, the text of which reads, "Individuality: Always remember that you are unique. Just like everybody else." Though both comforting and humbling, it makes a good point. No two of us *are* the same. The truth is, we cannot be fully described by one of four words. Each of us may carry characteristics of consumers, dreamers, owners, and stewards. We may present as one character type in one setting and a different type in another. For example, we might be an owner at work, a dreamer when it comes to our physical bodies, and a consumer in our churches or communities. There may be times and seasons when embodying one character type rather than another makes sense. We must be conscious and deliberate about when and how to utilize our particular resources and the difference we want to make with them. Understanding how you perceive and relate to people and the environment, as well as knowing your skills, abilities, passions, and dreams, is a critical first step in deciding how you want to engage with the world.

If you see parts of your life in which you have the mentality of a consumer, ask yourself, "Where can I invest? Where can I add time, talent, or treasure to what I already do and to how I engage with the world? What is that thing within me that is bigger than myself? What dream am I not dreaming? What hope do I secretly hold that I think is too big to realize?"

If you relate to the sidelined dreamer, ask yourself, "What have I convinced myself about the dream in my heart that keeps me on the sidelines? Where have I allowed fear to hold me back from engagement with the world and with others? To whom do I look for validation? Whose opinion matters more to me than my dream? What undeployed resources do I keep on the sidelines—and perhaps more importantly, *why*?"

Finally, if you are an all-in owner whose self-image is only as good as the last goal you've accomplished, ask yourself, "What is bigger than me? How can I step forth from doing what I'm good *at* to doing what is *good*? What are those things I possess that own me? What are the dreams that *don't* own me but should? Where is the meaning and purpose in my life that cannot be reduced to a spreadsheet or a to-do list? How can I take all that makes me *me* and make it about something more?"

CHAPTER 3

# A Mindset of Meaning

*"I fly because it releases my mind from the tyranny of petty things."*

**—Antoine De Saint-Exupéry**

Rolihlahla Mandela was born on July 18, 1918, in Mvezo, a tiny village nestled along the Eastern Cape of South Africa. It wasn't until he attended primary school that he was given the first name Nelson as a "proper Christian" name. Mandela's father was the principal counselor for the village king, which placed Mandela and his family in the upper echelons of his tribe. Nelson grew up roaming the countryside and playing with his friends in a carefree childhood existence, unaware that the color of his skin meant that the freedoms he experienced as a child were more illusion than reality.

Although his father died when he was only twelve, Mandela was able to attend good schools and even go to college, initially attending the University College of Fort Hare. In school, he became interested in African history and learned about how the arrival of the white people had disenfranchised and subjugated the native tribes in South Africa. The goal of restoring the rights and dignity of his people became a driving passion. Mandela wasn't able to complete his degree at Fort Hare; he was expelled for being part of a student-led protest of the mistreatment of Black South Africans. Instead of returning to his village after his expulsion, Mandela moved to Johannesburg and took several different jobs, including working in a law firm, before returning to school and earning his bachelor's degree from the University of South Africa. In Johannesburg, Mandela's interest in politics and social reform only intensified. It was there that he first joined the African National Congress (ANC) and helped found the organization's Youth League, quickly rising through its ranks.

In 1952, Mandela had his first brush with the law. He and a group from the ANC helped to lead a civil disobedience campaign against the system of apartheid, or racial segregation, that had been formally adopted by the country in 1948. Because of the political bent of the campaign, Mandela was charged under the Suppression of Communism Act and ultimately found guilty of "statutory communism," a crime for which he served nine months of hard labor.

After his release from prison, his college degree and prior work at a law firm enabled him to become an attorney. In 1953, he formed the law firm of Mandela and Tambo, the very first Black-owned law firm in South Africa. He began to rise in notoriety within the Black community of Johannesburg, a development that caught the attention of the South African government. Between 1956 and 1960, Mandela was arrested, imprisoned, and released multiple times, all while engaging in political activism and spreading opposition to apartheid. By the early 1960s, Mandela began to lose faith in Gandhi-inspired methods of peaceful civil disobedience. He came to believe that targeted acts of sabotage, worker strikes, and other aggressive actions were the only means that could bring an end to the barbaric system being imposed on the Black majority. Such antagonistic actions, along with his efforts to build and arm a resistance militia, ultimately led to his arrest in August of 1962.

Despite a three-hour opening speech at his trial that became known throughout the world as the "I Am Prepared to Die" speech— as well as international calls for his release—Mandela was convicted of treason in 1964. Although he could have faced the death penalty, he was instead sentenced to life in prison, where he would end up spending the next twenty-seven years. Initially subjected to abusive conditions and hard labor and limited to receiving one letter every six months, Mandela was eventually granted more privileges as he gained the respect of his wardens and fellow prisoners. Unbeknownst to him for much of his time in prison, Mandela remained the international face of the anti-apartheid movement, as highlighted by a 1988 tribute concert in London's Wembley Stadium, in honor of his seventieth birthday, viewed by more than 200 million worldwide. Mandela was eventually released from prison in 1990 and went on to be elected president of South Africa in 1994, after the repeal of apartheid.

One of the lesser known (but most remarkable) facts about Mandela is that he was offered his freedom on six separate occasions during his twenty-seven total years of incarceration. Each time, the offer was conditional, either on his leaving the country or on his agreement to refrain from ever speaking in public or engaging in any form of politics. Because the offers of freedom had a caveat, Mandela refused them each time. After rejecting one such conditional offer for release in 1985, Mandela said this:

> I cherish my own freedom dearly, but I care even more for your freedom. Too many have died since I went to prison. Too many have suffered for the love of freedom. I owe it to their widows, to their orphans, to their mothers, and to their fathers who have grieved and wept for them. Not only I have suffered during these long, lonely, wasted years. I am not less life-loving than you are. But I cannot sell my birthright, nor am I prepared to sell the birthright of the people to be free.

Mandela is a quintessential example of a steward. His transcendent core values were freedom, respect, and justice. Because he truly understood what freedom meant, he was able to recognize that the partial and conditional freedom offered to him was still a form of captivity. He knew that human beings are only *truly* free when they are *fully* free. That recognition meant he could not accept anything less than the fullest expression of the value (freedom) he had invested in during so much of his life. For him, true freedom was worth any price, even if it meant continuing to toil in a dark, cramped prison and being subjected to abuse and mistreatment. Mandela ultimately triumphed over injustice and caused the world to change because of his unwavering commitment to his inner values.

## THE MINDSET OF A STEWARD

As we established in chapter 1, a steward is someone fully invested in something bigger than himself or herself. They stand at the polar opposite of consumers. Stewards have learned that lift comes when you combine the skyward perspective of the dreamer with the forward focus of the owner, resulting in an upward trajectory that is full of both meaning and impact. Stewards experience this gift of lift because of the combined forces of their upward tilt, their forward drive, and their lack of weight. They aren't held down by anything—because they are owned by nothing but their purpose.

## FOUR POSSIBLE DESTINATIONS

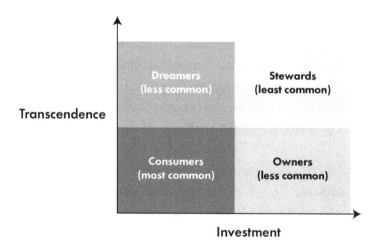

While every steward employs the two critical building blocks of investment and transcendence to carry them aloft, each steward is unique in how they express those two elements. Stewards are found in every walk of life, in every age group, and across the spectrums of religion, politics, culture, and creed. That said, there are four distinct ways in which stewards think and view the world that render them fundamentally different from the average mindset. It is because of these four unique mental approaches to life that stewards are so impactful in the world.

### 1. Stewards Know What They Value

In our book *Entrusted: Building a Legacy That Lasts*, my colleague Andrew Howell and I looked at seven disciplines that families who successfully transfer wealth (in all its various forms) generally practice. The first of those is a characteristic also found in stewards; they know who they are, what they value, and what they believe. This clarity of thought and understanding of themselves and their values is foundational to stewards. Aristotle said, "Knowing yourself is the beginning of all wisdom."

*City Slickers* is a 1991 comedy starring Billy Crystal and Jack Palance. Crystal plays Mitch Robbins, a middle-aged man searching for meaning and purpose in his life while on a cattle drive with his friends in the still-untamed American West. In one scene, Mitch is riding alongside Palance's character, Curly, talking about life, relationships, and love.

Curly stops, looks at Mitch, and asks him, "Do you know what the secret of life is?"

Mitch shrugs.

"No, what?"

Curly smiles, lifts one finger up, and replies, "This."

"Your finger?" Mitch responds, confused.

"One thing," Curly explains. "Just one thing. You stick to that, and everything else don't mean shit."

Looking perplexed, Mitch shrugs again and says, "That's great, but what's the one thing?"

"That's what you've got to figure out," replies Curly with an enigmatic grin.

As Curly's advice illustrates, clarity of conviction is essential to a life of meaning. But clarity of conviction does not mean conformity of thought. Stewards can have an enormous range of values, purposes, and beliefs. However, the key unifying element for them is that they are *consciously aware* of their values. Their meaning is rooted in their values and is always bigger than themselves. Their value-informed purpose is what drives stewards and helps them make intentional, consistent decisions. Taking stock of one's own values is a critical step to helping people understand the most valuable, meaningful, and motivational aspects in their personal lives, families, businesses, organizations, and communities. (This is such an important step in this journey, in fact, that Andrew and I devoted a second book, *Riveted: 44 Values That Change the World*, to unpacking just that.)

Stewards build a firm inner world and allow it to drive the way they engage with the outer world. They know who they are at their core, and yet they are completely free of themselves. In other words, they are not attached to an external image of themselves, and they don't require approval and validation from others. They define themselves by the next step in their journey, not by the last. Because they know their own values, beliefs, and principles, they are able to make clear decisions and take decisive action, and able to do so with a conviction most others lack. Oprah Winfrey expressed that, "I was once afraid of people saying, 'Who does she think she is?' Now I have the courage to stand and say, 'This is who I am.'"

### 2.    *Stewards Use a "Because/Therefore" Model for Life*

Because they have clear knowledge of who they are, what they value, and what they believe, stewards are able to use a distinctive model for thinking and decision-making. Most of the non-steward world operates within an "if/then" mindset. In other words, if I do $x$, then $y$ will happen, or if I do $b$, then the world/others will do $c$. This mindset renders life mechanical, transactional, and outcome-based. It leads to a contractual view of existence, even when the person doesn't explicitly know with whom or what they are contracting, or exactly what they expect as an outcome. The if/then model is expectation-based and self-centered. Success or failure, in each case, is based on the outcome (for the self) versus the expectations (*of* the self). Examples of the if/then model for life include the following:

- If I work hard at this task, then I will reap a substantial benefit.
- If I do this thing for my spouse, then he or she will act this way toward me.
- If I complete this task, then I will earn the respect of everyone in the organization.
- If I finish school, then I will get a high-paying job and have a great career.
- If I eat right and exercise, then I will be healthy and won't get sick.
- If I pray hard enough, then my child will be healed.

The if/then model is ubiquitous in modern culture, especially in the West, and it often guides our thoughts, actions, and attitudes without our even knowing it. At best, the if/then model leads to satisfied expectations—at worst, to unfulfilled ones. The problem with expectations is that they

- focus on the last step
- come with a desired or anticipated outcome built in
- are about what we anticipate receiving
- are about only what we can see—the tangible, observable side of life

- lead to ever-increasing expectations
- don't change anything

Expectations are also dangerous because they can lead to pride and hubris when realized, and frustration, inaction, and disappointment when not realized. One of the main reasons we often find ourselves in a state of anger or bitterness is that we are reacting to unmet expectations, either explicit or implicit.

In contrast, stewards have a "because/therefore" view of the world. This unique perspective makes life infinitely more relational, intentional, and transcendent. "Because" (transcendence) leads to "therefore" (investment). Transcendence is the driver, and stewards are the agents, investing their energies in something bigger than themselves. The expectations are on the self, not on the outcome: because I value *x*, I expect *myself* to do *y*. Examples of a because/therefore model include the following:

- Because I value compassion, I will therefore spend time volunteering in my community.
- Because I love artistry, I will therefore engage in acts of creative expression.
- Because I am an entrepreneur, I will therefore engage with the world through enterprise.
- Because I have faith, I will therefore act with certainty and clarity to express that faith.
- Because I value my health, I will therefore eat right and exercise regularly.

Unlike the if/then model of life, because/therefore propositions are values-based and, if implemented, will always bear fruit on some level. If you value compassion, for example, and use it as your driver, you will act with compassion, and those around you will receive the benefits of your actions. *You* will likely benefit too, but you will not *harbor expectations* that this will happen. You are performing the action for its own sake, in service of the larger value. Because your driver isn't rooted in an expected outcome, your acts of compassion will always result in achieving exactly what motivated you in the first place—to put your value out into the world. Your engine is meaning and your destination is open ended. You don't act compassionately because you are seeking a return of the favor. You act compassionately because you are compassionate. Your compassionate acts are an outward expression of your inner being and leave you grounded and complete, regardless of what happens as a result of your actions.

A because/therefore orientation also makes decision-making easier. *Because* Mandela valued true freedom (his transcendence), *therefore* he could not accept anything less than full freedom and so he continued to stay in prison (his investment). In fact, his driving value of freedom didn't end for him when he was finally released from prison; it simply morphed into new expressions of that value— new people to fight for and new changes to implement.

### 3.   *Stewards Know That Others Are the Key*

Stewards are unique in another way: they are both internally motivated and others-centered. Their inner world drives their decision-making and sets the course for their lives, but they always act with an eye toward the outer world. People, passion, and purpose drive stewards far more than profits, pride, and position do. Mandela could not accept his own freedom when he knew it would come at the expense of others failing to gain theirs.

As humans, we know the importance of others, or at least we know the importance of *saying* that others are important. Our desire to try to instill a sense of other-centeredness in our children from an early age is nearly universal. A recent study found that a staggering 96 percent of parents said they believed that raising caring, ethical, others-centered children was "very important, if not essential" to their children's having a quality life. In addition, parents highly valued their children being "honest, loving, and reliable."[48]

While these aspirational values may be present among virtually all parents, the message that's being received by children may, unfortunately, be quite a different one. In the above study, titled, *The Children We Mean to Raise: The Real Messages Adults Are Sending About Values,* by Harvard's Making Caring Common Project, researchers looked at the messages parents *think* they are giving to their children as compared to the messages kids say they hear. Although the study found that most parents and teachers consider "caring for others" a top priority for their kids—one that ranks above achievement—here is what the children said:

- The youths surveyed reported that their parents and teachers were more concerned about achievement (54 percent) or happiness (27 percent) than caring for others (19 percent).
- Youths were three times more likely to agree than disagree with this statement: "My parents are prouder if I get good grades in my classes than if I'm a caring community member in class and school."
- Hard work was consistently ranked as a far higher value than kindness or fairness.
- Of high school students, 57 percent agreed that that "in the real world, successful people do what they have to do to win, even if others consider it cheating."[49]
- When polling middle and high school students, 30 percent reported being bullied, and over half of the girls in those grades reported experiencing at least one episode of sexual harassment. These statistics tend to indicate that "caring for others" is not a practiced value for many schoolchildren.

The problem is that not only are children hearing something different from what parents and teachers think they are communicating, but they are also getting the wrong message about *how* achievement and happiness are actually attained in life. Most of us intuitively think that in order to achieve in this world or to be happy, we should *focus* on achievement and happiness—and should encourage our kids to do the same. And yet the research indicates that this approach may not be creating the outcomes we desire.

With respect to focusing on achievement, the researchers discovered the following:

> Putting too much emphasis on one's own accomplishments may . . . undermine children's empathy. In our data, ranking achievement first was associated with low levels of empathy. . . . Ironically, this pressure is not even likely to achieve what it's intended to achieve. Children who are subjected to intense achievement pressure by their parents in affluent communities don't appear to outperform other students. Further, a good deal of research now points to the importance of social and emotional capacities in achievement and professional success, capacities that are too often neglected in the press to achieve.

> In other words, focusing on achievement as an end in itself doesn't produce the results we want and can actually inhibit the development of empathic capacities that may, in fact, lead to the achievement we were hoping for. In a similar way, focusing on happiness not only fails to accomplish its intended results, it can also make matters worse. It may seem strange to suggest that youth can be too focused on their happiness or that parents can be too focused on their children's happiness. But too much focus on happiness, just like going overboard on achievement, can imperil both children's moral development and, ironically, their happiness.

One of the biggest problems with a focus on happiness is that it creates within us a very self-focused perspective of the world. At its very essence, individual happiness is about happiness for the individual, which can sometimes (or often) come at the cost of others. At the very least, it can come without considering the impact that such a focus has on others. The researchers found that when parents prioritized their children's happiness over more others-centered values like empathy, their children were "less likely to do what's right, generous, or fair both in making mundane decisions such as whether to pass the ball to a friend, and when in the throes of high-stakes conflicts between their own welfare and that of others, such as when deciding whether to risk standing up for a friend who is being bullied."[50] Students of parents who focused on the happiness of their children over caring for others were, unsurprisingly, less likely to volunteer or tutor and also much less likely to develop critical coping mechanisms that come from dealing with personal adversity. Ironically, the reduction in service to others and lack of coping skills ultimately resulted in lowered perceived levels of happiness in the children over time.

Instead of focusing on happiness itself, the researchers suggest that parents should help their children develop meaningful relationships and positive coping skills for handling trials and difficulties. They also recommend "reducing [children's] self-occupation by, for example, engaging them with principles and projects larger than themselves." In other words, the research indicates that the steward's mindset of combining transcendence with others-centeredness is actually the best combination with which to succeed in attaining both happiness and achievement.

Finally, the practice of including others in our lives produces a host of ancillary benefits besides bringing us greater peace, happiness, and achievement. In the book of Ecclesiastes, King Solomon talks about the difficulty of toiling alone. He then says this:

> Two are better than one, because they have a good return for their labor: If either of them falls down, one can help the other up. But pity anyone who falls and has no one to help them up.

Also, if two lie down together, they will keep warm. But how can one keep warm alone? Though one may be overpowered, two can defend themselves.

In this passage, Solomon enumerates four specific benefits that people can bring to each other by working in partnership. First, they can increase their productivity by employing teamwork. Second, they can lift each other up when one of them falls down and needs a hand. Third, they can care for each other and provide for each other's physical (and emotional) needs. Fourth, they can defend each other against life's struggles, attacks, and trials. What a great recipe for a lasting relationship! Work together, pick the other up when one is down, care for each other, and have each other's backs. Interestingly, Solomon ends this passage with the following: "A cord of three strands is not quickly broken."

Solomon doesn't explain this transition from two to three, but one interpretation is that the third cord represents the relationship itself. Individuals have self-driven goals, wants, and needs. But relationships exist at a higher level than the individual and have their own requirements and rewards. A marriage or a business partnership is an entity unto itself, one that both draws strength *from,* and gives strength *to,* the individual parties involved. Relationship is the third cord because it transcends each person and renders the union of the two stronger than the sum of its parts. One plus one, bonded together, equals three. Stewards recognize this and understand that relationships provide not only our first and best source of motivation and positive intentionality but also a powerful reservoir of comfort, support, and strength.

### 4.  Stewards Are Guided by Both Present and Future

Finally, one of the most distinctive characteristics of stewards is their connection with the timeline of life. They see their role as a temporary one. They know that life is on a clock. This perspective makes them both forward thinking and openhanded, and allows them to take on goals and projects they cannot accomplish alone or within their own lifetimes. Stewards aren't concerned only with how their group or organization functions while they are alive and in charge; they look to the life of their business, family, organization, community, and even their country, *after they are gone.* In short, stewards care more about their successors than they do about their own personal success. This perspective makes them intentional about how they allocate their time, talent, and treasure, and also makes them generous when it comes to investing their resources and encouraging others to do the same.

The Cathedral of Our Lady towers about the city of Strasbourg, located along the Rhine River in the northern part of the Alsace region of France. With its single tower reaching 466 feet, between 1647 and 1874, the cathedral was the tallest building in the world. Although the history of the site goes back to 12 BC, the construction of the current edifice as it stands today was begun by architect Erwin von Steinbach in 1277. The building itself is overwhelming both in its size and details, with hundreds of figures blanketing the exterior and ornate stained-glass windows providing the light for the equally imposing interior.

Early on, Erwin realized that the grand vision for what he saw the site becoming could not be completed during his lifetime. After his death in 1318, the work was taken over by his son Johannes von Steinbach and eventually his grandson Gerlach von Steinbach, who oversaw the construction until his death in 1372. Subsequent architects continued the work until it was finally completed in 1439, more than 160 years after Erwin began the task. Had he, or any of the many others who worked on the imposing, ornate structure, sought to build something that they could have completed during their lifetime, the world would have been robbed of a truly towering achievement and one of the finest masterpieces of Gothic design in the world. Each of them saw themselves as part of something, both literally and figuratively, bigger than themselves.

Likewise, Cincinnatus, Washington, and Mandela saw beyond themselves and realized that power and authority are meant to last only for a limited period of time. As a result, they looked down the road to what would be best for their countries after their own personal influence had ended. This type of forward thinking impacted how and why they came to power and how they left. These men also realized their fights—for values such as freedom, self-governance, and equality— were bigger than themselves and, therefore, that their own personal benefit should never be a driving force in their decision-making. The perspective Cincinnatus, Washington, and Mandela shared, while relatively rare, is the only one that can lead to cohesion, lasting vision, and sustainability in organizations and nations.

Susan B. Anthony was born into a Quaker family on February 15, 1820, in Adams, Massachusetts. Anthony's father treated his sons and daughters equally and taught all of them business principles and the importance of self-reliance and self-sufficiency. Although her father was a strong supporter of suffrage for women, Anthony's first foray into social reform did not stem from her belief that women should have the right to vote but rather from her conviction that they should receive equal pay for equal work. She operated the family farm for several years of her early life before focusing exclusively on social reform. Through her work, she came into contact with Elizabeth Cady Stanton, who was a strong voice in the women's rights movement, and the two became lifelong friends. Stanton was a strong intellectual force and gifted writer, and Anthony was a talented orator and organizer. They became powerful allies and a force to be reckoned with on the national stage. As Stanton once described her relationship to Anthony, "I forged the thunderbolts; she fired them."[51]

Although she is best known for being a vocal leader in the suffrage movement,[52] as well as in the temperance movement and the fight for the rights of Black Americans, Anthony's greatest struggle was perhaps in fighting for the right of women to speak. On multiple occasions throughout her life, she was either prevented from speaking at gatherings and conventions where men were present, or else she spoke anyway, sending those gatherings into chaos. Anthony once remarked, "No advanced step taken by women has been so bitterly contested as that of speaking in public. For nothing which they have attempted, not even to secure the suffrage, have they been so abused, condemned, and antagonized."[53]

Realizing that the fight for equal rights and treatment of women would require more of a movement than simply a moment, Anthony used her organizational skills to found and operate a number of influential groups. She established the Women's Loyal National League in 1863 (focused on ending slavery and advancing women's rights), the American Equal Rights Association in 1866 (focused on passing a Constitutional Amendment to give women the right to vote), the National Woman Suffrage Association in 1869 (which led to her arrest in 1872 when she had the "audacity" to attempt to vote[54]), the International Council of Women in 1888 (a multinational effort to bring rights to women on a global stage), and the Rochester branch of the Women's Educational and Industrial Union in 1893 (which worked to raise funds so that women could be admitted to the University of Rochester).

Anthony's legacy and impact as a steward for human rights was lasting and profound. Although the Nineteenth Amendment, which guaranteed women the right to vote, was not passed until 1920, fourteen years after her death, it became widely known as the Susan B. Anthony Amendment. After achieving its objective, the National Woman Suffrage Association morphed into the League of Women Voters, which still thrives today. Anthony became the first woman to adorn United States coinage when her image was placed on a $1 coin in 1979. In 2016, the United States Treasury discussed adding her face to the back of the $10 bill, along with Elizabeth Cady Stanton and other notable American women. And the place where she was arrested for voting in 1872? It now bears a statue of Anthony that commemorates her act of civil disobedience.

Anthony is an example of someone who was fully invested in something bigger than herself. She knew what she valued, she embraced a because/therefore model that guided her on her path, she invested in the lives and hopes of others, and she held fast to a vision of what the world could be in the future, not just for women but also for the whole of humanity.

## FOUR POSSIBLE DESTINATIONS

**Stewards**
(least common)

⚙️ **Investment:** Deeply invested

🔍 **Focus:** Outward

🕐 **Time:** Present and future

🏰 **Focus:** Upward

➡️ **Driver:** Purpose

👁 **Perspective:** Entrusted

👥 **Portion of Population:** Rare

CHAPTER 4

# The Power of Counterbalancing

*"The Guide says there is an art to flying,"*
*said Ford, "or rather a knack. The knack lies in*
*learning how to throw yourself at the ground and miss."*

**—Douglas Adams, *Life, the Universe and Everything***

**B**alance has become a buzzword of the twenty-first century. In our fast-paced, overscheduled lives, where the typical way of dealing with our growing list of needs and wants is to simply double down and work harder and acquire more, the reactive call for balance has sounded its alarm in virtually every facet of our culture. Our already-overworked brains are now bombarded with messages proclaiming the need to balance our time, our schedules, our meals, our workouts, our hormones, our relationships, our pH levels, our hobbies, and our obligations. We take probiotics to balance our antibiotics, and depressants to balance our stimulants. Balance has even made its way to how we are supposed to train our dogs. (Yes, a fierce debate rages in the dog-training community about the merits of "balanced dog training," which employs a combination of positive reinforcement and aversion techniques to elicit the desired behaviors in our best friends—who themselves all seem to have become balance-bred with some portion of poodle.[55])

Perhaps nowhere has the notion of balance become a hotter topic than in the search for that utopian state of being known as "work-life balance." On any given day, the lists of top-selling businesses and self-help books are peppered with titles promising practical paths to attaining this mythical goal of life equilibrium. Whether it's working just four hours a week, managing your business in one minute, or taking the monumental step of not working one day a week, we have become inundated with strategies for bringing balance to work and life. We've reached the point where about the only thing we don't want to balance or moderate is our politics.

In response to our "the only thing better than more is even more" culture, it is natural to think of balance as simply the process and practice of moderation. We've come to view balance as an attempt to titrate our efforts, energies, and resources in order to achieve this moderated state we consider so necessary and valuable. Unfortunately, for many of us who strive to live with intentionality and impact, this search for balance ends up feeling like the mere avoidance of extremes by doing things in a half-hearted or mediocre way—which hardly seems worth the effort (or non-effort, as the case may be).

Stewards, as we discussed in the last chapter, view life through a different lens and with a different perspective. Their unique mindset allows them to see beyond the binary approach of a "more or less" optionality and impels them to seek something more powerful than balance.

They seek counterbalance.

## WHAT IS COUNTERBALANCING?

Counterbalance means "to weigh against with an equal weight." Counterbalances are used in a wide range of everyday devices, such as elevators, cranes, drawbridges, and even metronomes. The purpose of a counterbalance, or counterweight, is to provide a strong opposing force so that a machine can more effectively accomplish the task for which it is designed. Counterbalances provided the power behind the castle-destroying trebuchets of the Middle Ages and have been used for hundreds of years to keep the Leaning Tower of Pisa from becoming the Horizontal Tower of Pisa.

The idea of a counterbalance has even been proposed as the basis for a "space elevator." The elevator car would be parked at one end of a giant cable anchored at the equator, and the counterweight would be positioned a mere 22,000 miles, give or take, above Earth and beyond its gravitational pull. Such an elevator could theoretically be used to transport space explorers to and from planet Earth without the need for rockets.[56]

Far from acting to limit or diffuse its opposing force, a counterbalance is meant to bring added strength, focus, and direction to the force it is countering.

The concept of a counterbalance is not limited to mechanics. In food, the primary "forces" of flavor include salty, sweet, sour, and bitter.[57] *Counterbalancing* these primary flavors with one another allows a cook to enhance and strengthen, rather than merely tone down, each of the flavors. Adding salt, for example, acts to enhance the taste of sweet (salted caramel ice cream, anyone?) and to moderate bitter so that its flavor can be better appreciated.

Counterbalancing is also used in the culinary arts to pair two entirely different things, such as drink and food. Sommeliers spend entire lifetimes trying to find wines that perfectly complement great foods in order to heighten the impact of both the food and the wine. Rather than acting against each other or muting each other's impact, an artful red wine from the Capurso Winery, for example, makes a perfectly cooked *tagliata* taste even better, and vice versa. The combination of steak, salt, lemon, and Parmigiano-Reggiano cheese provides a tapestry of counterbalancing effects designed to bring out every note and flavor hint within the vineyard's signature red, the Diavolo Rosso.

So, what if instead of our doing a vital activity *less*, we found counterbalances that allowed us to *amplify* our actions and energies? Such an ability to bring enhanced power and perspective to life pursuits is one of the main benefits of being a steward. Stewards balance transcendence (their why) with investment (their how) and, by using each as a counterbalance, allow the force of each to magnify the other. And because stewards adopt the long-term perspective that goes along with taking on something bigger than themselves, their lives acquire a deliberate cadence, which allows them to move at a measured and intentional pace without burning out.

## THE IMPACT OF COUNTERBALANCING

In traditional artillery weapons, a spring hammers the firing pin in a shell to ignite a small explosive charge that in turn ignites a propellant in the larger part of the shell. Employing Newton's third law of motion, the rapidly expanding gas from the explosion pushes against the back of the barrel and propels the bullet forward. The barrel also gives direction and spin to the bullet, helping guide it to its intended target. Although the projectile exits the end of the barrel with astonishing speed, the fastest it will ever move is at the point of initial explosion. From that microsecond onward, friction against the inside of the barrel and against the atmosphere outside it, combined with the pull of gravity, immediately conspires against the bullet to reduce its speed. This deceleration also works to slowly erode the bullet's ultimate impact, in keeping with Newton's *second* law, which says that force is equal to mass times acceleration.

A rail gun, on the other hand, has an entirely different mechanism. Rather than using an explosive force from inside the projectile, a rail gun uses a magnetic field powered by an immense electrical current to act as the accelerant and to propel the metal-encased projectile forward. Power flowing *up* a positive rail and *down* a negative rail produces a vector field within the gun that launches the projectile. Instead of decelerating, the projectile within a rail gun actually accelerates as it travels through the barrel in a frictionless and perfectly centered manner, ultimately reaching speeds of more than six times the speed of sound as it exits. Because the projectile of a rail gun is traveling three to seven times faster than one fired from a traditional gun, its kinetic impact is anywhere from twenty-five to fifty times greater.

Like perfectly paired magnets, the twin forces of transcendence and investment help stewards avoid the friction, pull, and distortion of the other force, resulting in focused direction and enhanced impact. The force of investment keeps a steward from becoming just a dreamer, and the counterbalancing force of transcendence helps them avoid the trap of becoming merely an owner. The combination of transcendence and investment also works to create purposeful direction for the steward while generating a real-world impact that is multiplicative, not merely additive. This is evident in the lives of the notable stewards we have looked at so far.

George Washington began his public service career in the mid-eighteenth century as a special envoy during the French and Indian War and ended it as the first president of the United States. Susan B. Anthony took her family's passion for social reform and magnified it exponentially, becoming one of the most influential voices for change in the nineteenth century. Martin Luther King Jr. combined his extraordinary verbal gifts with his opposition to the evils of segregation to become the most powerful American orator of the twentieth century.

The ability to embrace the push-pull of the countervailing forces of transcendence and investment is the hallmark of the steward and leads to three unique and powerful benefits.

## 1.   Counterbalancing Leads to Meaning and Purpose

In the field of positive psychology, a major focus of research today is on the concepts of meaning and purpose and how they affect the way we view and approach life. Often used interchangeably, the terms *meaning* and *purpose* actually have distinct definitions that are fairly hotly debated within the positive psychology community. For the "purpose" of our discussion of the terms (as they relate to the life of a steward), I'll posit these definitions: Meaning is the place outside ourselves where our personal notions of value, virtue, and love reside. Purpose is the gravitational pull we feel *toward* that place—in our hearts and souls—and our ongoing drive to get there. Put more simply, meaning is found in *what* we love, and purpose is our *drive to express* that love through our actions.

Researchers have come to the general consensus that purpose should be defined as follows: "Purpose is a stable and generalized intention to accomplish something that is at once personally meaningful and at the same time leads to productive engagement with some aspect of the world beyond the self."[58] As you may note, within this modern definition of purpose, we find both of the building blocks of stewards. Transcendence involves the focus on "some aspect of the world beyond the self," and investment relates to the "intention to accomplish something," which leads to "productive engagement." The arrow of purpose draws momentum from the countervailing forces of transcendence and investment, which propel stewards through the consumer quadrant and help them avoid the schism of becoming either a dreamer or an owner. Purpose ultimately leads a steward to a life that is "personally meaningful."

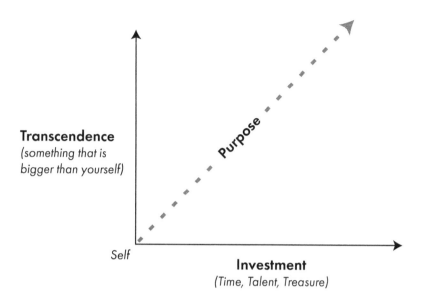

While both purpose and meaning may contain different definitional elements depending on who is defining the terms, there are some things we can say with certainty about the paired concepts. First, purpose is far-reaching and not merely a means to an end. Purposes that can be achieved relatively quickly or easily are actually *goals.* There is nothing wrong with a goal as long as it is seen as a step and not a destination. Good grades are not a purpose, nor is losing five (or twenty-five) pounds. A good grade or a slimmer waistline may get you closer to fulfilling your purpose of a successful or healthy life, but they are not purposes in and of themselves. When life is reduced to a series of short-term goals, it results in a start-stop type of dynamic that is ultimately unfulfilling.

For many, the purpose they pursue as a result of their marriage of transcendence and investment is unachievable in their lifetime. As we have discussed, Susan B. Anthony and Martin Luther King Jr. are but two examples of stewards whose purpose outlived them. While seeking to accomplish mighty things beyond their personal ability, they nevertheless powerfully advanced the ball from where they picked it up and, in doing so, laid the groundwork for future generations of difference-makers.

Second, neither purpose nor meaning should be confused with happiness. The past thirty years of psychological study have seen a tremendous increase in the study of happiness, as well as (to a lesser extent) in the study of meaningfulness. In 2013, researchers from Florida State University, the University of Minnesota, and Stanford University sought to tease out the differences, if any, between the two.[59] To do so, they surveyed nearly 400 people on their perceptions of both happiness and meaningfulness. While they generally found a correlation between the two—people who described themselves as happy felt as though they were living lives of meaning and purpose and vice versa—they did discover some key areas where the two concepts materially diverged.

Among the key differences between people who lived happy lives and those who lived meaningful ones were the following:

- Health, wealth, and ease of life were all elements of happiness, but were not actually correlated with meaning. In other words, respondents who felt meaning and purpose in life were distributed across the spectrum of financial resources and personal health situations and reported being able to find meaning even in the midst of challenging circumstances. The political prisoner engaged in a hunger strike for a passionate purpose might not be described as "happy" but might be living a highly meaningful life.

- Happiness was seen as based on one's current situation, while meaning incorporated elements of past, present, and future. Respondents' happiness level tended to rise and fall based on their current circumstances, while their sense of meaning was significantly less impacted by the moment. Those with higher levels of meaning viewed life as more of a continuum than a single point in time or a destination.

- Happiness was seen as flowing from receiving, while meaning was seen as a product of giving. According to the researchers, happiness seems to correlate with receiving tangible things from others, whereas meaning comes from an investment of time and effort in someone else. For example, receiving a birthday gift from a friend may lead to an increased feeling of happiness, while spending time *caring* for someone else, like a child or a sick person, can lead to greater feelings of meaning.
- Meaningful lives more often involved difficulty. Those with higher levels of meaning also reported higher levels of stress, worry, and even anxiety. The researchers theorized that taking on difficult, challenging, or even seemingly impossible tasks may lead to higher levels of meaning, but may also produce lower levels of happiness, due to the difficult personal costs (or investments) required.
- Self-expression correlated more with meaning than with happiness. Respondents with higher levels of meaning tended to do things to express their identities, creativity, and uniqueness. Their higher sense of personal meaning allowed them to more easily be who they are and express their true selves.

The question of whether one should strive to live a meaningful life or merely a happy one is not a new one. Aristotle wrote often of the concept of *eudaimonia,* which literally translates to "well spirit." While it was traditionally thought of as an ancient Greek version of happiness, modern philosophers have come to view the concept with a more expansive definition that includes living a flourishing life of meaning, purpose, and virtue.

Ralph Waldo Emerson certainly had a strong opinion as to whether one should seek a life of happiness or one of meaning and purpose. He said, "The purpose of life is not to be happy. It is to be useful, to be honorable, to be compassionate, to have it make some difference that you have lived and lived well."[60] Note, by the way, the concepts of transcendence and investment embedded in Emerson's view of the life well lived.

Finally, purpose and meaning lead to direction and impact. As noted earlier, meaning is the destination, and purpose is the drive *toward* the destination. Like the horizon, meaning is a place to which you can never actually arrive. But while meaning and purpose cannot be found on a map, they *can* be used as a compass. The transcendence we gain from meaning guides us in our personal investment of time, talent, and treasure, the three of which in turn combine to supply us with both purpose and directionality.

In the book *The Culture Code*, author Daniel Coyle dissects the ways in which highly intentional groups and organizations use purpose to set direction and measure progress. In his words, "High-purpose environments are filled with small, vivid signals designed to create a link between the present moment and a future ideal. They provide the two simple locators that every navigation process requires: Here is where we are, and Here is where we want to go."[61] The powerful benefit of using meaning and purpose as a directional force is this: once you know where you are and where you want to go, you are left with only the question of how you plan to get there. We will discuss the impact of stewards on culture in more detail in chapter 6.

2.   *Purpose Brings Freedom and Clarity*

One of the biggest problems with both consumers and owners is that their desire to acquire actually leads to a form of enslavement. Like the biblical rich young ruler who owned more property than he could walk away from (which makes one wonder who owned whom), the accumulation of material possessions can as easily become a burden as it can become a blessing.[62] This issue is especially acute in the United States, where, according to becomingminimalist.com[63]

- The average home contains 300,000 items.
- One-quarter of homes with two-car garages don't have room to park cars in them.
- There are more than five times more storage facilities than Starbucks locations, with enough space in total to provide standing room for every single person in the United States.
- Women today have more than three times as many complete outfits (thirty) as did American women from the 1930s (nine).
- People spend more on clothes, jewelry, and watches than on higher education.
- There are more shopping malls than high schools.
- Over the course of an average lifetime, women spend eight years shopping, and men spend nearly half a year looking for misplaced items.

This feeling of burden that comes from possessing and managing all this stuff has led in large part to the minimalist and tiny-home movements that are sweeping much of the Western world. While just 10 percent of consumers currently consider themselves minimalist, nearly two-thirds of Americans want to become more minimalist in the future.[64]

Like owners, stewards are fully invested; they are "all in" with their time, talents, and treasure. What separates stewards from owners is that while stewards may own assets, they are not owned by those assets. Thanks to the counterbalancing force of transcendence, stewards recognize that freedom doesn't come from owning many things but rather from the feeling of not being owned by anything. Their lives are based in contentment with what they have and discontentment with the trials, struggles, and tribulations of others. They realize that freedom is not a virtue or even a destination; rather, it is the living result of practicing transcendent values and virtues such as faith, generosity, sacrifice, and others-centeredness.

It is this conception of personal freedom that counterintuitively allowed Nelson Mandela to spend twenty-seven years in prison as a man who was free in his soul. It is also what allows stewards to fully invest in their chosen values while simultaneously transcending ownership itself.

Gail Miller's decision to transfer the ownership of the Jazz was made infinitely easier by her perspective. Because she didn't view herself as the team's owner, the notion of "giving it away" was not painful. She and her husband, Larry, acquired the team with a clear purpose, which was to provide a meaningful and lasting resource to the community as a whole. As a result, her subsequent decisions on how to run the franchise and how to transfer its ownership to a trust and beyond were simply the next logical steps in accomplishing that greater purpose. It would have been as illogical for her as a steward to try to personally benefit from the team's value as it would be for an owner to consider giving away an asset of such high value.

This ability to transcend ownership leads to one of the most common characteristics of a steward: generosity. It is so much easier to give away something you don't "own"—and especially something that doesn't own *you*. For stewards, generosity is more than just what they do; it's who they are in their hearts.

The very notion that someone is "kind-hearted" or would "give in a heartbeat" may be more than casual hyperbole. In a 2017 study conducted by researchers at Anglia Ruskin University and Stockholm University, generous people were found to be literally in tune with the beat of their own hearts.[65] In their experiment, the researchers had subjects play a game that involved sharing their winnings with other, unknown participants. The winnings equated with actual financial benefit in the real world. In a second part of the study, subjects were asked to listen to various sounds and to determine, without feeling their own pulse, whether the sounds were in time, or out of time, with their own heartbeats. During this experiment, participants' heartbeats were recorded using an ECG machine.

Those participants who were better at detecting the rhythm of their own heart gave away more winnings on average than those who were poorer at the skill. As the researchers concluded,

> It may be that an emotionally-charged situation—such as deciding whether or not to give money away—causes a change in heartbeat. This bodily change may then bias decision-making toward the generous option in those people who are better at detecting their heartbeats. These findings suggest that, in some sense, people "listen to their heart" to guide their selfless behaviours.[66]

### 3.   *Freedom and Purpose Are Good for You*

Finally, the purpose and freedom that derive from counterbalancing transcendence with investment are actually good for both your soul and your body. Various studies have shown that those who possess a greater sense of meaning or purpose in life live longer than those who don't. Purposeful people also have reduced morbidity, fewer heart attacks, and reduced incidences of Alzheimer's disease and cognitive impairment as they age.[67]

Purpose and meaning can help us deal with adversity and struggle as well. After controlling for other factors, researchers in one study were able to predict better outcomes for people recovering from knee replacements based solely on their sense of purpose.[68] Patients who displayed higher levels of purpose in life had better mental health, which in turn led to better coping skills, such as more active engagement with follow-up treatments and physical therapy. As a result, these patients had superior results from their procedures.

While many studies have shown the mental health benefits of adopting meaning and purpose, and the concomitant negative effects on the psyche when these transcendent elements are absent, few studies have looked at what happens to a person's *physical* body when transcendence is lacking. In one study that did examine that connection, researchers studied the blood of 236 cardiac patients at the University of Michigan—in particular, their levels of Interleukin 6 (IL-6).[69] IL-6 is a molecule that plays a key role in the inflammatory response crucial to wound repair. Conversely, chronically elevated IL-6 is often associated with depression and cardiac disease resulting from arterial inflammation. In their study, the researchers found that individuals in the midst of religious struggle, defined as a "crisis-related existential conflict," had elevated levels of IL-6 and poorer outcomes to their cardiac issues. In other words, those who struggled to have a positive relationship with either a higher power or a transcendent universe were at a physical disadvantage in dealing with cardiac disease and related treatments.

Beyond being personally beneficial, a life of meaning and purpose is far more sustainable than an aimless existence and can help one avoid the plethora of problems associated with burnout. As discussed in chapter 2, hedonic adaptation is the principle that while positive and negative experiences can impact our happiness level in the short term, we have a natural tendency to return to our prior level of personal happiness.

To demonstrate this, researchers at the University of Chicago and Northwestern University gave one group of students $5 a day to spend on the same item for themselves each day, for a week.[70] Unsurprisingly, the students reported higher levels of happiness the first day of their newfound "wealth" than the prior day, but that happiness level reverted back to the average by the end of the week.

The second group had more unexpected results. With this group, the researchers also gave each participant $5, but now the subjects were required to spend that money on someone else. As with the first group, this second group reported increased levels of happiness on day one. What was different, however, was that this second group did not have the typical hedonic return to the mean. Instead, their reported levels of happiness stayed elevated throughout the week. In other words, unlike the first group, they did not habituate to the positive feeling, thus muting its felt impact. The researchers tried to tease out a dozen different variables to explain the difference, but ultimately came to the conclusion that "giving" is simply fundamentally different from "getting." We become inured to receiving, but giving continues to reward us.

## COUNTERBALANCING IN ACTION

Sanduk Ruit was born into a poor, illiterate family in Olangchung Gola, a small village high on the mountainside along the Tibetan border of Nepal. The second of six children, he was one of only three to make it to adulthood; three of his siblings died from diseases and medical issues that would have been largely treatable in most other places on the planet. Ruit took these losses personally and turned his heartache into an abiding resolve to ensure that everyone, especially the people of his community, had access to modern medicine. He realized that the poor and marginalized are the ones who typically suffer the most in the world today. And so, despite growing up a seven days' journey from the nearest school, which meant staying far from home, he fully invested himself in education, graduating not only from high school and college, but also from medical school.

As a medical student, Ruit was drawn to ophthalmology, owing in large part to the fact that an estimated one million people in Nepal suffer from some form of blindness, 90 percent of which is treatable. Ruit studied in India, Australia, and the United States before eventually training under, and teaming up with, Australian ophthalmologist and professor Fred Hollows.[71] This partnership led Ruit to focus on cataract surgery, the only cure for cataracts, which are the main cause of blindness in Nepal.

Although the cost of intraocular lenses, a necessary component of modern cataract surgery, was only $250 to $300, Ruit realized that even at that price, few if any of the blind in Nepal could afford them, and that raising the needed funds would have been virtually impossible for most. So, instead of giving up or accepting a more modest impact, Ruit devoted himself to finding new ways to develop and manufacture the lenses and simpler ways to implant them in patients. The result of his efforts was to bring the cost of these lenses to less than $3, nearly a 99 percent reduction in cost. He did that, at least in part, by moving the manufacturing to Nepal, which brought jobs and expertise to his country as well.

Ruit's innovative efforts didn't end with the lenses; he also pioneered faster and more effective methods for cataract surgery, methods that have proven so successful they have been emulated throughout the West. Over the course of his lifetime, Ruit has personally performed more than 130,000 eye surgeries and has helped oversee efforts that have reduced blindness in Nepal by 70 percent. He has traveled and performed surgery in many countries beyond his own borders, including North Korea, where he conducted more than 1,000 surgeries and trained local surgeons in his techniques.[72]

Ruit's story is a great example of how stewards live their lives. His transcendent values of compassion and empathy, especially for the poor, led him to make a significant personal investment in becoming a doctor despite his extremely challenging life conditions. He was then able to see lives directly impacted by the work he did, which in turn fostered increasingly more personal investment in his work. The counterbalance of transcendence and investment allowed him to live a targeted life of purpose and meaning that changed the collective wellness of not only his own country but also the entire world.

Ruit's payoff for this life of counterbalance has come not mainly in monetary riches or in the accumulation of things. Rather, it has come in the expressions on the more than 100,000 faces that have looked back at him over the years each time he removed their eye bandages. As Ruit describes it, "I've seen thousands, but each patient's story touches my heart. And it is the expression of these patients who have been blind yesterday, and suddenly they come out and see everything in front of them, see people they loved, and they change the perspective on life in a fraction of a second."

CHAPTER 5

# Becoming a Steward

*"If you can't fly, then run.*
*If you can't run, then walk.*
*If you can't walk, then crawl,*
*but by all means, keep moving."*

**—Martin Luther King Jr.**

O f all the virtually limitless uses for the internet, one of the more engaging and debate-inducing ones is the compilation of lists, especially top ten, twenty-five, fifty, or one hundred lists. Although list-making dates back to the origins of human writing, it really took off with the computer age. Today, virtually every area of our life has published lists that enable us to categorize and place value on the people, places, and things around us. Famous list-makers include individuals like Benjamin Franklin, Richard Blackwell, and David Letterman; magazines like *Forbes*, *Time*, and *People*; and organizations like the FBI, *Billboard*, and the *New York Times*.

When it comes to who tops the lists of historical figures, whether it's a list for the most famous, most influential, most impactful, or most popular, one name almost always comes in at the summit: Jesus of Nazareth. Depending on the theme of the list, runners-up typically include the likes of Isaac Newton, Albert Einstein, Aristotle, Muhammad, Leonardo da Vinci, Mahatma Gandhi, Nikola Tesla, Napoleon, and William Shakespeare. Contrary to the pronunciations of John Lennon, even the Beatles routinely come in second, at best, to the teacher from the Middle East.[73]

In 1999, *Time* magazine not only devoted a cover story to Jesus as he entered his third millennium of influence on the planet but also decided to eliminate him from consideration for their Person of the Century because they felt he might win and that naming him would go against the "spirit" of the voting.[74]

If you've ever told someone to "go the extra mile," "follow the straight and narrow," or be a good Samaritan; warned someone against "casting the first stone" or about "wolves in sheep's clothing"; told someone not to "live in a house divided" or "cast pearls to swine"; or talked about "the blind leading the blind," "living or dying by the sword," or "watching the signs of the times," then you've drawn from the teachings or sayings of Jesus.

One of the more remarkable but lesser-known facts about the famed carpenter from Nazareth, however, is that, although he is generally recognized as one of the greatest teachers of all time, Jesus rarely gave straight answers to questions. Far more often, he would return questions with questions. In the book *Jesus Is the Question*, author Martin B. Copenhaver analyzed the four gospels of Matthew, Mark, Luke, and John[75] and discovered that in those four biographical accounts, Jesus asked a total of 307 questions, covering a wide variety of topics. In return, Jesus was asked 183 questions. Of those, depending on how you count them, Jesus directly answered between three and eight of them. That's right. Jesus was all about the questioning.

This method of returning questions with questions was not unique to Jesus, of course. It was a form of teaching common among Jewish rabbis and teachers of the day and is still the traditional way of teaching in Judaism. In fact, a customary observance of Passover in the Jewish community involves having the youngest person in attendance asking a series of questions about the evening and why things are being done a certain way. The purpose of this tradition is to encourage inquiry as a means of learning. So ubiquitous is this Judaic practice of questioning that there is a joke within the Jewish community:

Student: Rabbi, why do you answer every question with a question?

Rabbi: Why shouldn't I answer every question with a question?

Many other cultures have also honed this practice of questioning as a means of discovery. Socrates was so famous for this technique that the so-called Socratic method is still used today in schools, colleges, and universities as a form of instructional dialogue often focused on morality and enlightenment. Questioning has been powerfully employed throughout human history to help increase understanding across religions, cultures, and countries. Part of the reason questions are so powerful is because imbedded within them are two of the most powerful elements of relationship building: humility and respect. When you sincerely ask a question, you are in essence saying, "I lack something that I think you possess. Will you share that with me?"

Although question-asking has been used for thousands of years to foster relationships, knowledge, and wisdom, it has lost a great deal of popularity in today's world. Today we live in the information age, where what we know is valued far more dearly than whether or not we know *ourselves* or are known by others. Meaningful questioning takes time and requires investment, relationship, and listening, all of which are in short supply today. Questions are about the *learner*, and we live in a world that is often far more focused on the *learned*. Too many of us seek followers who are hungry to download our information, advice, or instruction, and not compatriots with whom we can share our time, our thoughts, and our attention.

So, the "question" for many of us in the modern era is this: If Jesus came with a message to impart, why did he ask so many questions? Put another way, how could Jesus be recognized as one of the most influential teachers of all time if he answered only a handful of questions?

If I were Jesus, I would probably leave the question there, but because I'm clearly not, I will venture an answer. Like many of the greatest teachers throughout human history, Jesus realized that knowledge, facts, and data merely *in*form, but questions and stories *trans*form.[76]

Our phones have access to virtually all the knowledge humanity has compiled throughout its time on Earth. We can search and instantly find the answer to almost any question we want to ask, whether it's about geography, history, math, language, culture, science, or even just the lyrics to that song that is nagging at us. And yet with all this information at our literal fingertips, we often struggle with knowing who we are, what we value, and what we believe. Perhaps we need to fight the urge to dole out answers, or to search for answers ourselves, and instead start asking important questions of ourselves and others.

**The reality is that while data, knowledge and information inform, it is questions and stories that transform.**

## GOT QUESTIONS?

In chapter 1, I laid out the definition of a steward—someone who is fully invested in something bigger than himself or herself. So, if that is the definition, then it raises two critical questions that must be answered before one can hope to become a steward:

- *What is it that I hold as bigger than myself?*
- *How will I fully invest myself in that bigger thing?*

The first question—*What is it that I hold as bigger than myself?*—is by far the most important one in your journey to becoming a steward, because it will lead you (or your business or organization) to the next question, the one of action. You cannot know how to effectively and positively mobilize your resources unless and until you know what drives, motivates, and emboldens you in a transcendent way.

That said, the answer to the question is far more elusive than it might seem. The only way to determine what is truly meaningful, purposeful, and transcendent to you is through asking yourself a series of difficult and demanding questions.

In ancient Greece, the Oracle at Delphi attracted sojourners from far and wide, seeking answers to their questions, especially questions about their future endeavors and about journeys or quests they planned on taking. The oracle would in turn provide cryptic answers to the travelers, who would then spend their time on their adventures trying to understand the answers they'd been given and how those answers might possibly relate to their current situation. All this was done purposefully by the oracle to provoke further self-inquiry within the traveler. On the wall, within the sacred inner reaches of the temple, where only the oracle and her attendants were allowed, was written perhaps the best reply to any question a person could ask: "Know thyself."

On the pages that follow, you will find a lot of questions. A *lot*. And I encourage you to answer each and every one of them. This chapter is perhaps the most important one in the book because if you invest the time, effort, and resources in this work, it will yield the most fruit. You will discover *your own* answers, not mine and not someone else's. If you truly desire to foster the steward within you, or if you desire to become a desperately needed steward in this world, prepare to think carefully on the questions that follow so that you can truly "know thyself." This process of questioning yourself takes time, but because time is the most powerful of the three types of investment, it will likely produce enormous value in return.

The investment of your time and effort now will save you potentially years of wasted effort and resources, and allow you to live a centered, strategic, and purposeful life focused on the authentic passions of your heart. Spend time thinking, journaling, and talking with others about every question posed here. You never know which one will spark within you the clarity of thought that will reveal your inner North Star in your life as a steward.

## A QUESTION OF VALUE

Let's start with questions of value. One of the surest ways to come to know what is potentially transcendent for you is to understand what you value or hold dear.[77] Our *values* are those core elements in our lives that give us juice, empower us to stand our ground, bring tears to our eyes, or move us to act. While some of our values flow from our life stories and our reactions to great or terrible events in our lives, other values are simply products of who we are and who we've always been.

Values aren't *feelings,* like peace, joy, happiness, or even contentment. Such passing emotions are actually by-products of our real and enduring values, such as justice, mercy, connection, creativity, loyalty, determination, and integrity. Values point us toward the ideal, the virtuous, and the excellent. Knowing your own core values can be a powerful way to start articulating what is personally transcendent to you.

Here are some questions to ask yourself in the value realm. (Note: The questions that follow can also be found in the appendix, where you can, and should, take the time and effort to try and answer them for yourself.)

- *What is the greatest compliment I could ever receive? That I could ever give?*
- *What virtues bring tears to my eyes when I see them embodied? Why?*
- *Whom do I admire the most, and what is it about him or her that I admire?*

- *What does the world need now more than ever?*
- *What is one of the best ways to express love?*
- *What part of my story am I most proud of?*
- *What gets me excited in life?*
- *When and where am I the most myself?*

## A QUESTION OF TRANSCENDENCE

Embedded within these questions of what we love and care about is the importance of other people, an essential component of transcendence. If your transcendence doesn't include a deep, positive, meaningful impact on and connection to others, it's not actually transcendent, because you're not thinking about anything bigger than yourself. Other-centeredness must always be an essential part of your search for something bigger than yourself.

Here are some questions to ask yourself in the transcendence realm:

- *Who are my others?*
- *Does what I love positively impact others? If so, how?*

As mentioned in chapter 1, Abraham Maslow, developer of the famed hierarchy of needs, believed that the highest of all human needs was self-transcendence—freedom *from* yourself, not merely *for* yourself. To help people identify what is of transcendent value beyond themselves, Maslow developed his own set of thought-provoking questions to ask: [78]

- *What is the good life?*
- *What is the good man? The good woman?*
  *What is the good society, and what is my relation to it?*
- *What are my obligations to society? What is best for my children?*
- *What is justice? Truth? Virtue?*

- *What is my relation to nature, to death, to aging, to pain, to illness?*
- *How can I live a zestful, enjoyable, meaningful life?*
- *What is my responsibility to my brothers?*
  *Who are my brothers?*
- *What shall I be loyal to? What must I be ready to die for?*

## A QUESTION OF PRIORITIES

Once you figure out what you love and what you value, it's time to take a long, hard look at the *number* of values you are juggling and their relative priority. Augustine of Hippo was a theologian and philosopher who lived between 354 and 430 AD, and for him, the question of what we value was really a question of what we love. According to Augustine, "For when we ask whether somebody is a good person, we are not asking what he believes or hopes for, but what he loves." Augustine believed that human virtues are actually expressions of love and that human failings result from a lack of love. We are what we love.

Augustine also recognized that we can love many different things, but that we have ascending priorities when it comes to our various loves. Author Timothy Keller explains Augustine's thinking this way:

> You may say that you believe in social equality and justice and think that you do, but if you make business decisions that exploit others, it is because at the heart level you love your own prosperity more than your neighbor's. In short, what you love most at the moment is what controls your action at that moment. [Augustine writes,] "A body by its weight tends to move toward its proper place. . . . My weight is my love: wherever I am carried, my love is carrying me." You are what you love.[79]

Augustine observed not only that the heart's loves have an order to them, but also that we often love the less important things more and the more important things less. Therefore, unhappiness and disorder in our lives is caused by the disorder of our loves. A just and good person "is also a person who has [rightly] ordered his love, so that he does not love what it is wrong to love, or fail to love what should be loved, or love too much what should be loved less (or love too little what should be loved more)." [80] What does this mean in practical terms? There is nothing wrong with loving your job, but if you love it more than your family, then your loves are out of order, and you may ruin your family. Or if you love making money more than you love justice, then you will exploit your employees—again, because your loves are disordered.

The question then becomes not just what things do you love, but also in what order of priority do you love them? To help identify the priority of your values, passions, and loves, ask yourself the following:

- *What do I love? Make a quick list.*
- *For each thing I love, why do I love it?*
- *Is it something temporary?*
- *Is it a person? If so, do I love* who that person is *or* how they make me feel?
- *Is there anything transcendent about what I love?*
- *Is what I love bigger than myself or simply something I can buy, experience, or consume?*
- *What loves of mine take precedence over other loves?*
- *What loves should move up my list?*
- *What loves should move down my list or be taken off altogether?*
- *Is there something behind what I* think *I love that is actually capturing my heart?*

## A QUESTION OF FOCUS

If you intend to live the life of a steward, you will also need focus. Specifically, you will need to home in on those few essential things in life that compose your transcendence. Stewards, rather than taking a shotgun approach, are focused and intentioned on a small number of priorities—usually just one to three. And that is what makes stewards' lives impactful.

To illustrate this, let me share a story. A few years ago, I worked with a very successful family office that had recently sold a major asset that had been the focus of decades of hard work and effort. It was an asset that carried with it a tremendous name-brand recognition and value in the marketplace. Because of this asset, this family was known as being in the very upper echelon of their particular industry.

As they prepared to launch into the next phase of their business, I took them through an exercise to help them understand and articulate the values that would transcend who they were and what they valued as a company. After considering many questions and engaging in powerful conversations, they ended up settling on three values that they felt had marked their brand in the past and that they wanted to continue to mark it moving forward:

- Loyalty: They wanted to be loyal to one another and to their clients and customers.
- Integrity: They wanted everything they did to have a sound ethical backbone.
- Excellence: They wanted to take on new initiatives only if such projects could be executed with the excellence their brand required.[81]

Later in the day, they started to debate the merits of a particular investment they had been contemplating for months. The project had substantial upside as well as the potential for very solid cash flow. However, it was going to require expending a large amount of time and effort in a location geographically remote from their current operations. And so, they were a bit stymied as to whether or not to proceed with it.

I asked them a single question to help them clarify their thinking: "Can you do this new proposed project with excellence?"

"No," the CEO of the family office immediately responded. "It's decided, then. We aren't going to do the project."

While they could have made significant profits, they realized that they couldn't execute the project with the excellence they wanted their brand to represent. When viewed through the lens of their three transcendent values, their decision-making became clear, straightforward, and simple. By not investing in this project, they were able to keep their energy and resources available for those projects and opportunities that checked off all three of their essential values.

Ask yourself these questions regarding focus:

- *Am I trying to value too many things?*
- *Which of my values should rise to the top?*
- *If I could be known for only three things, what would they be?*
- *Is my transcendence actionable (i.e., can I do something to advance its cause)?*

## THE QUESTIONS OF JESUS

Finally, regardless of your beliefs about or perspective on Jesus of Nazareth, there are some powerful questions among the 307 he is reported to have asked that apply to anyone and everyone, even today:

- *What am I looking for?*
- *Whom am I looking for?*
- *Why am I afraid?*
- *Where is my faith?*
- *Why do I doubt?*

Perhaps his first question is the most powerful and profound. What are you looking for? We've all had the experience of going into a room to search for something, only to forget what it was we were looking for. We instantly cease our activity because we inherently recognize there is no point in continuing the search until we remember what it is we want to find. Unfortunately, in life, too few of us know what we are looking for, and as a result, we find ourselves either frozen in place or consigned to wandering aimlessly from moment to moment. Being on a conscious discovery quest, on the other hand, gives shape and direction to every moment of our lives.

Knowing what you are looking for is critical for another reason: If you don't know what you're looking for, how will you know whether or not you have found it? Many people find out too late that they actually had what they were looking for all along and simply failed to recognize and appreciate it until it was gone.

## THE VALUE OF STORYTELLING

As mentioned earlier, Jesus taught primarily through questions and stories. In fact, most of those sayings of his that we use every day came from stories he told. In her fantastic book *The Power of Meaning: Finding Fulfillment in a World Obsessed with Happiness*,[82] author Emily Esfahani Smith details what she sees as the four essential elements for a life of meaning. The first three—belonging, purpose, and transcendence—are all easily understandable and make sense as we think about them. The fourth, however, may seem surprising: storytelling.

As any expert communicator knows, we humans are built for storytelling. If you want to instantly capture someone's attention, you need only say the words "Let me tell you a story." Storytelling not only connects people together, but it also helps us to understand ourselves, others, and the world around us. Here's how Smith explains it:[83]

Our storytelling impulse emerges from a deep-seated need all humans share: the need to make sense of the world. We have a primal desire to impose order on disorder—to find the signal in the noise. We see faces in the clouds, hear footsteps in the rustling of leaves, and detect conspiracies in unrelated events. We are constantly taking pieces of information and adding a layer of meaning to them; we couldn't function otherwise. Stories help us make sense of the world and our place in it, and understand why things happen the way they do.

Stories can also help us to make sense of, or even find redemption in, the trials and difficulties we face in life. They help us to gain perspective on what we've been through and to see how our darkest moments may have brought us strength, endurance, or peace.

Accordingly, as you go through this chapter and think through the questions, also look back at your own life story. Analyze the successes, the failures, the trials, and the triumphs. What themes do you see? What are the through lines that become obvious only upon reflection? What are the pivotal moments in your life—the turning points—that you may not have even realized were pivotal at the time? Consider telling your story to one or more friends and asking them to tell you their story. In this process of storytelling, you may find out more about yourself than you ever knew.

## THE ANSWER

Once you've gone through these questions and arrived at some level of understanding and clarity, it's critical that you turn that insight into something you can articulate and implement. Whether you call it your personal mission statement, vision statement, statement of values, or a term of your own choosing, you need to write down your twenty-second elevator speech on why you are on this planet and how you intend to leave it different than how you found it. This mission or vision statement can be a phrase, a sentence or two, or even a full paragraph. It should be something that you can easily explain to yourself and to others, and something to which you can hold yourself accountable. If you dare (and stewards often do), you can even ask others to hold you accountable to acting upon it.

Because your "mission statement" should be both transcendent and ideal, it should not focus on a concrete goal that you can or will achieve. The paradox of stewards' lives is this: They constantly seek to achieve the unachievable and to reach a place they cannot ever arrive at. Paradoxically, that knowledge that they're never going to reach the finish line leads to peace. Why? Because the pressure is off. Stewards know transcendence is about a direction, not a destination, and this knowledge allows them to live a life driven by purpose rather than performance.

In the appendix is a summary of the questions above as well as a place to write out your own personal transcendence. I've also included in the back of this book a copy of my own personal transcendence, not as something for anyone else to follow, but as an example of what it is for me.

**DETERMINING INVESTMENT**

Once you have articulated what is transcendent and directional for you, the second question is, *How will I fully invest myself in that?* Those who are able to clearly state what is bigger than themselves, but who then fail to answer this second question and act on it, often end up as dreamers, not stewards. That's because it is impossible to bring value to our transcendence without investment and cost. Without cost—whether that be time, talent, or treasure, or a combination of the three—no value is ever really created.

That said, being a steward is not necessarily about doing more, accomplishing more, or adding more to your resume. It is not about piling more stress and pressure onto your life. Being a steward is about being fully invested in something bigger than yourself. It's about your purpose. Purpose is your *how,* and it flows from your *why.* Stewardship, though it leads you to full engagement, actually results in greater peace, perspective, and contentment because the thing that is bigger than you is . . . BIGGER THAN YOU. You won't ever be able to fully accomplish it, so there is no fear of failure. And that is a liberating thing.

As outlined in chapter 1, the three things you can invest are your time, your talent, and your treasure. One simple way to begin thinking about how you might invest in your transcendent values is to consider what you would do if you were allocated even just a bit more of each of these three resources. For example, if you were given just three extra hours per week, how would you invest those hours in what is bigger than yourself? If you were able to improve or develop just one additional talent, what would it be and why? And finally, if you were given just a few more financial resources, how would you spend those funds toward your *why?*

This is how I will invest my extra time:

_____

_____

_____

This is the talent I will invest in improving or developing:

_____

_____

_____

This is how I will invest my additional monetary resources:

_____

_____

_____

While I cannot give you three extra hours a week, unfortunately, or develop any of your talents, or even give you additional money,[84] the reality is that each of us *can* prioritize our lives in such a way as to free up all three of these things. As Mark Twain said, "To change your life, you need to change your priorities." Figure out what could be cut from your schedule (Netflix, anyone?) and from your budget (Starbucks, anyone?), and then use those resources toward your answers above.

## THE HARD WORK OF A STEWARD

The life of a steward is a constant feedback loop between the internal and the external. The external informs the internal; the internal affects the external. Constant plowing, planting, sowing, and repeating is required. Stewards must be self-reflective, thoughtful, and directed on the inside so they can live lives of clarity, purpose, and impact on the outside. Answering the questions in this chapter, if done right, will likely be a daunting task, but it should result in a clarity of purpose and vision that creates powerful movement in your life. As Mae West once famously said, "I never said it would be easy; I only said it would be worth it."

# CHAPTER 6

# The Essentials of Culture

*"Angels can fly because they take themselves lightly."*

**—Gilbert K. Chesterton**

*T*he *Tales of Mother Goose* was a collection of stories curated by Charles Perrault and originally published in France in the seventeenth century. The collection contained eight fables based upon folktales that had been orally passed down for generations throughout Europe. Perrault put his own unique spin on these stories, based on his personal life experiences and his imagination. *The Tales of Mother Goose* became so popular that Perrault became known as the modern-day father of the fairy tale genre. Included in the collection were enduring classics such as "The Sleeping Beauty in the Wood," "Little Red Riding Hood," "Puss in Boots," and "Little Thumb." Perhapsthe most famous story, however, was "Cinderella" (or "Cendrillon" in the original French), which was subtitled "The Little Glass Slipper."

Known the world over, "Cinderella" tells the story of a girl whose mother dies and whose father marries a cruel stepmother with two daughters of her own. With her father essentially absent from her life,

Cinderella—or "Cinderwitch," as she is called by her stepsisters—is harshly treated by her new family. Nevertheless, her outer beauty is surpassed only by her inner grace, and she accepts her fate with strength and charm. Eventually cared for by a fairy godmother who helps her gain entry to the king's ball, she meets the prince of the land, who proceeds to fall madly in love with her. Unlike many of the more modern versions of the story, where both the stepmother and stepsisters get the comeuppance they deserve, in Perrault's version, Cinderella not only forgives her stepfamily but also ensures their place in the castle and the kingdom. Her story is a tale of forgiveness and the power of character in action, matched with the beauty and grace to create something even better (think counterbalance).

Not only has "Cinderella" been remarkably enduring, but it has also been adopted into, and adapted by, countless cultures throughout the world. According to Martine Hennard Dutheil de la Rochère's book *Cinderella Across Cultures*,[85] there were 345 known versions of the story in existence by the end of the nineteenth century (well before Disney got hold of the tale), and there are more than 500 today. Although each version contains common connections to the basic story, unique elements are found within each that reflect the perspectives and values of the various storytellers' cultures.

The Brothers Grimm's German rendition of the story, for example, is about Aschenputtel, and their tale of good versus evil features a far more gruesome, if not fitting, ending. In it, Aschenputtel's mom dies, and a magical tree sprouts over her grave. The tree takes the place of the fairy godmother and helps Aschenputtel make it to the ball to meet the prince. The stepsisters attempt to fit their feet in the glass slipper by cutting off their toes, which results in the shoe being filled with their blood. After Cinderella is reunited with the prince, birds come and peck the eyes out of the stepsisters, leaving them blind and haggard.

Taking a less harsh tone, "The Little Red Fish and the Clog of Gold" is the Middle Eastern tale of an Iraqi fisherman's daughter named Maha.[86] In this story, the young woman's mother also dies. Her father remarries a woman who comes to despise Maha because of her good nature and character, which stand her in stark contrast to her own daughter. One day, Maha spares the life of a fish that turns out to have magical powers, and the fish, in turn, helps Maha attend a bride's banquet incognito, dressed in the finest of clothes and, of course, in a pair of gold clogs. At the end of the evening, she rushes home to avoid being discovered by her stepmother, only to lose one shoe in the river. A prince recovers the shoe, tracks down Maha, and they fall madly in love. The story emphasizes the belief that Allah never lets kindness go unrewarded.

"Cinderella" has even made its way into modern-day American sports, where athletes and teams that overcome tremendous odds are often referred to as "Cinderella stories." One of the greatest of these is the 1980 United States Men's Hockey Team which was comprised of a ragtag group of college athletes. The team went on to beat the prohibitively favored USSR team stacked with top professionals to win Olympic gold in the now famous Miracle on Ice.

Each version of the "Cinderella" story is impacted by the culture in which it lives, and reflects the values and ideals that culture considers important—whether that be forgiveness, justice, kindness, or even simply the hope and joy that come from seeing someone overcome staggering odds against them.

## STEWARDS AND CULTURE

As noted in the prior chapters, stewards are distinctive individuals who effect a lasting, powerful impact on the world around them. One of the most important ways stewards do this is through their influence on culture. Culture, at its essence, is the understood beliefs, behaviors, attitudes, and actions of a specific group of connected people. As Daniel Coyle describes it in *The Culture Code*, "Culture is a set of living relationships working toward a shared goal. It's not something you are. It's something you do."[87] Said another way by researchers Boris Groysberg, Jeremiah Lee, Jesse Price, and J. Yo-Jud Cheng, "Culture is the tacit social order of an organization: It shapes attitudes and behaviors in wide-ranging and durable ways. Cultural norms define what is encouraged, discouraged, accepted, or rejected within a group."[88] Culture exists not only within formal organizations, but also within families, communities, and nations.

A consideration of culture is critical to a proper understanding of life as a steward because culture exerts such a powerful yet unseen force on who we are and what we do. Because stewards are part of various groups, each with its own unique culture, they realize there are only two essential choices: affect your culture, or be affected by your culture. Tell the story, or be influenced by the story. Stewards recognize that culture is the effect of the collective *we* on one's chosen purpose. Stewards know that if they can foster a positive, healthy, and vibrant culture around them, they can magnify the purpose they have adopted. If they cannot, they will end up swimming upstream and spending much of their energy fighting the current, rather than making forward progress in their battle for meaningful change.

My wife and I love cycling together. We often spend hours riding in the mountains, in the valleys, and on the bike trails of the beautiful state of Utah. Sometimes, when we are fortunate, we will have a tailwind behind us, which gives us amazing help as we pedal along. The world around us becomes quiet and still because our bikes are matching the cadence of the invisible yet powerful force of the wind. The tailwind makes us feel buoyed and strong. By contrast, few things are more disheartening to bicyclers than headwinds. A headwind can slow down a cyclist and force them to exert substantially more energy than otherwise required. Like a tailwind or a headwind, the culture of your environment plays a significant role in how quickly you can accomplish the various expressions of your stewardship, and whether or not you can accomplish them at all.

In *The Leader's Guide to Corporate Culture*, Boris Groysberg and his fellow authors note four key attributes of culture:[89]

1. **Culture is shared.** It cannot exist solely within a single person. It resides in shared behaviors, values,

and assumptions because it is quintessentially a group phenomenon. Wherever two or more individuals come together in any type of group, you have culture.

2. **Culture is pervasive.** Culture permeates multiple levels of thought and behavior and has broad influence on a group or organization. It is found in every part of the organization, and in every member, and it manifests itself in group behaviors, rituals, physical environments, stories, and—as with "Cinderella"—even in legend.

3. **Culture is enduring.** Culture informs the thoughts and actions of group members over the long term. Shaped by experience, culture also begins to *affect* experience because it attracts those who find comfort in the particular expression of that culture and repels those who do not. As a result, it tends to become more engrained over time.

4. **Culture is implicit.** Despite the subliminal nature of culture, people are hardwired to recognize and respond to it instinctively. When new people are exposed to a group, they begin to sense its cultural norms and seek to either adopt or avoid the group as a result.

Four Key Attributes of Culture

Culture is shared

Culture is pervasive

Culture is enduring

Culture is implicit

Simply put, culture and its effect on each of us is unavoidable and should never be overlooked. You might have clear vision as a group and the best structure and strategy possible, but if you don't effectively address culture, you will spend (waste) significant resources dealing with (battling) culture, and you will likely fail to fully achieve your objectives. As Peter Drucker once said, "Culture eats strategy for breakfast."

## FOUR PILLARS FOR BUILDING CULTURE

Stewards who desire to create purpose, based on transcendence and investment, within their organizations realize that building strong culture is key. To accomplish this, stewards focus on four key pillars. Each of these pillars follows the path of the steward because each involves both meaningful investment and transcendent purpose. By developing these four pillars within a group, the group acquires the potential to produce more stewards and, in turn, to promote greater meaning and purpose for the individual members of the group and for the group itself.

Before starting to read about these pillars, think of a group you are a part of, whether it's your family, circle of friends, business, or organization. Then, as you finish reading about each pillar, give some thought to the questions at the end of the section and how you would answer them for that group. Also, consider asking those questions of fellow group members, and see if you get the same or different answers.

## COMMUNICATION

Communication is the first pillar of culture-building and is one of the most powerful tools for a steward who wants to meaningfully affect the culture of their organization. Groups that regularly engage in healthy communication reap several benefits. They are able to resolve conflicts more effectively, they allow others to express themselves so that everyone can be known and understood, and they clarify what needs to be known by the group. The formula for communication from the perspective of a steward is as follows:

*Respectful Sharing + Respectful Listening = Communication*

In this formula, sharing is the transcendence, and listening is the investment.[90] Sharing takes what is inside of us and externalizes it, while listening is an investment of time and attention in another person. Both require a deep level of respect, and both require a high degree of humility. Effective communication is impossible without both of these elements. As Carlos Ruiz Zafón said, "Fools talk, cowards are silent, wise men listen."

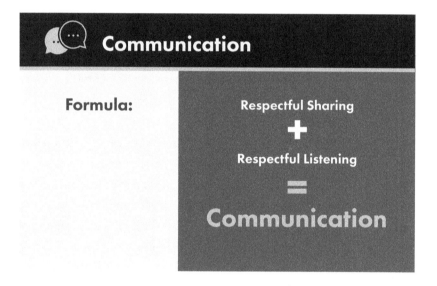

In one of the most-watched TED Talks on the importance of communication, journalist and author Celeste Headlee offers ten basic rules for how to become a better listener and communicator. For her, the key is not to *act* like you are listening by doing outer things like making eye contact or nodding. Rather, the secret to listening is to actually *be* a good listener. Her recommendations draw from skills and strategies employed by professional interviewers:

1. **Don't multitask.** Beyond setting aside your phone and turning off your computer, be present in the moment. Don't be thinking about a prior conversation or future event. Direct all of your brain's focus toward the person in front of you.

2. **Don't pontificate.** Conversations should not be seen primarily as opportunities for sharing your ideas and opinions with someone else. Go into each conversation with the attitude that the other person is correct and you are uncertain. This allows you to relinquish your personal agenda and actually listen, as opposed to merely waiting to be heard.

3. **Use open-ended questions.** Like a good reporter, a good conversationalist starts with the basics of who, what, where, when, why, and how. Let the other person describe their circumstance or emotions in their own words, as opposed to feeding them words to agree or disagree with.

4. **Go with the flow.** Let go of thoughts that pop into your mind, and stay with what the other person is saying. Don't steer the conversation back to previous points when the person talking has moved on.

5. **When you don't know, say you don't know.** We live in a complex, specialized world, and it's okay not to know something or, heaven forbid, not to have an opinion. You will gain more respect by admitting your lack of knowledge than by acting as if you have an answer for everything.

6. **Don't equate your experience with someone else's.** Every experience is unique, both in its details and in the emotions it produces in the experiencer. If someone is going through a difficult circumstance, don't tell them how you went through "the same thing," because, well, you didn't.

7. **Try not to repeat yourself.** When you repeat yourself, you tend to come across either as condescending or as someone who isn't paying attention.

8. **Stay out of the weeds.** Stated another way, don't worry about the minutiae. Often, we waste time and energy in a conversation trying to remember information that is not really relevant to the subject at hand or to the emotions that are being conveyed.

9. **Listen.** The art of listening is perhaps the most important and least developed skill in the modern world. Listening is the greatest gift we can give another person; it allows us to communicate respect and interest. But because we can listen at more than double the rate at which we can talk, slowing down and listening can be a challenge. As a result, too often we are more focused on what we are going to say next than on what someone is trying to communicate. Stephen Covey put it this way: "Most people do not listen with the intent to understand; they listen with the intent to reply."[91]

10. **Be brief.** When it's your time to talk, getting to the point quickly allows you to focus on what really matters and not get sidetracked by what doesn't. Brevity also allows the other person more time to speak and share.

If you really want to improve your communication skills, ask others in your group(s) the following questions (and, of course, listen to what they say):

1. What could I do to be a better communicator with you?
2. What makes you feel listened to or heard?
3. What are the best ways I could share my thoughts with you and hear your thoughts in return?
4. Is there something you'd like me to know, or is there something you would like me to share with you?

## COHESION

The next pillar of culture-building is cohesion. Cohesion is the sense, within a group, of being a united whole, or the movement toward creating such a unified whole. Groups that successfully foster stewardship have members who feel they are an important part of the group, who forge bonds with other members of the group, and who treat each other with respect. The steward's formula for cohesion is as follows:

*Engaged Relationship + Clarity of Purpose = Cohesion*

Here, relationship is the investment, and purpose is the transcendence. The difference between simply having a relationship and having a sense of cohesion is the addition of purpose. Unfortunately, too many families and organizations fail to add purpose to their relationships, which ultimately detracts from the impact of the group, as well as from the group's longevity.

Society today is perhaps more diverse than ever before. We live in a multicultural world that lacks many of the constructs that formerly, for better or for worse, bound us together. Widespread religious views, common ethnicity, and even similar political perspectives rendered the world of yesterday a more homogenous place. The variety of differences in today's world is perhaps starker than at any point in human history. Beyond the obvious cultural differences that separate us, we are also far more different *generationally* than at any time in the past. That is because of the increasing rapidity of change in our era. Take four random people, one born in 1940, one in 1960, one in 1980, and one in the year 2000, and you will find they have lived fundamentally different lives with vastly different sets of experiences. This level of diversity, which strengthens us in so many ways, also creates a significant impediment to cohesion.

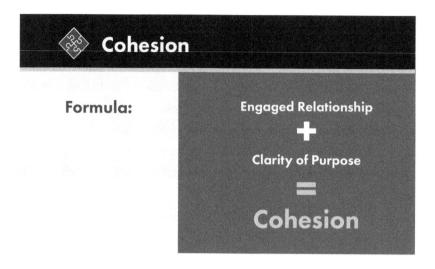

One of the most important things to understand about cohesion, and why stewards focus on both relationship and purpose, is that there are actually two types: social cohesion and task cohesion. Social cohesion is the emotional connection a group feels on a relational level—their sense of friendship, closeness, and caring. People in groups with high social cohesion enjoy spending time together and feel a strong attachment to one another. Task cohesion, on the other hand, is the connection a group feels when they work together on a shared task or common challenge. Task cohesion has to do with a group's commitment to completing a specific goal or objective. Both social cohesion and task cohesion rely on the same critical building block—commonality.

From a social standpoint, cohesion can be developed by taking a step back from the myriad differences that divide us and finding shared values, experiences, or associations. Identifying areas where we can agree, or positive experiences we can share, can help develop social cohesion within a group. Whether it's the shared value of creativity, the common experience of visiting Italy, or simply a sports team to rally around, discovering common denominators in a group can be a great way to build social cohesion. While social cohesion can be a powerful force, it is not without its potential negative side effects, which can include a desire for conformity (so that you appear to be an integrated member of the group), groupthink, and over-socializing—which can hamper a group that desires to be productive in addition to sociable. Also, social cohesion tends to be easy for extroverts but may be more difficult for introverted individuals, which can further limit its effectiveness.

The second way to build cohesion is through task cohesion, which relates to the commitment to achieve a goal in a collective manner. Task cohesion can be found in sports teams, military platoons, purposed businesses, visionary nonprofit organizations, and even within certain highly intentional families and groups of friends. There are two potential benefits to focusing on task cohesion in addition to, or even in place of, social cohesion.

First, task cohesion typically results in higher performance than social cohesion. Researchers Albert Carron, Steven Bray, and Mark Eys discovered a strong correlation between task cohesion and performance.[92] They studied high-level college basketball and soccer teams in Canada and found that teams with a stronger sense of cohesion tended to significantly outperform those with lower levels of cohesion. Beyond achieving better performance, highly cohesive, task-oriented groups interact more with each other, develop more supportive and communicative climates, are friendlier and more cooperative, and have a greater belief that their personal and group goals are being met than low-cohesion groups.[93]

Second, task cohesion can overcome many of the differences that can stymie groups attempting to rely on social cohesion. Instead of straining mightily to find similarities within a diverse group, which can become especially trying in larger numbers, focusing on a meaningful task can naturally bring groups to a high state of cohesion. The six-time world champion Chicago Bulls of the '90s are a classic example.[94] While the team was certainly built around Michael Jordan, who was at the time the face of the entire NBA and one of the most recognizable people on the planet, it also included the quiet-but-forceful Scottie Pippen, the flamboyant and over-the-top Dennis Rodman, the choirboy-looking Steve Kerr, the "Croatian Sensation" Toni Kukoc, and their Zen-master coach, Phil Jackson. While clearly a disparate group of individuals, they had a singular purpose that brought them successful cohesion. Strong task cohesion is also found in the military, where individuals from a wide variety of backgrounds, lifestyles, beliefs, and perspectives find that working together, especially in perilous situations, brings a sense of cohesion that can last a lifetime.

 **Types of Cohesion**

| | |
|---|---|
| **Social Cohesion:** | Social cohesion is the emotional connection a group feels on a relational level: their sense of friendship, closeness, and caring. People in groups with high social cohesion enjoy spending time together and feel a strong attachment to one another. |
| **Task Cohesion:** | Task cohesion, on the other hand, is the connection a group feels when they work together on a shared task or common challenge. Task cohesion has to do with a group's commitment to completing a specific goal or objective. |

**Both social cohesion and task cohesion rely on the same critical building block: commonality.**

If you want to take a steward's perspective on building a lasting sense of cohesion within your family, workplace, or community, think of the particular group you want to focus on, and ask yourself the following questions:

1. What experiences, values, or beliefs do we share?
2. If you can't think of any of the above, what new experiences could we share?

3. What common values could we identify?
4. Is there a shared task we could take on as a group or a shared goal we could work to achieve?

## IDENTITY

While purpose can be a powerful tool for building cohesion, it can be accomplished only when there is clarity. Within the context of a group, clarity isn't about simply understanding yourself but also about understanding each person in the group and the group identity as well. That is why the third pillar of culture for stewards is identity. Like the overlapping section of a Venn diagram, group identity is the sweet spot in which the individual *me* of each person becomes an integral part of the collective *we*. The steward's formula for identity is as follows:

*Knowing Who You Are + Knowing Who You Want to Be = Identity*

For this pillar, knowing who you are is the transcendence, and knowing who you want to be is the investment. Knowing who you *are* is definitional—what kind of person are you today, and what drives and motivates you? Knowing who you *want to be* is aspirational. It is about who you desire to be tomorrow. Taken together, these twin elements of identity provide both the map and the compass. In chapter 5, I provided a series of questions you can ask yourself to come to a deeper understanding of your own identity. For identity to infuse itself in the groups you are a part of, you will need to go through a similar questioning process on a collective basis.

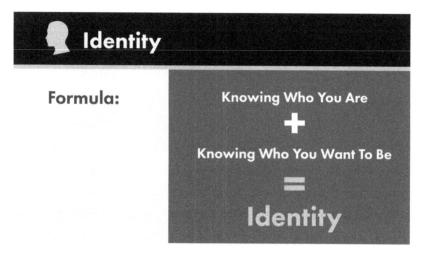

Groups that successfully develop stewards, and allow them to live the most impactful lives possible, know what matters to their members individually and collectively. They have clear expectations for each member of the group, they can articulate the group's core values, and they have a strong sense of purpose. Again, here's how Coyle describes it in *The Culture Code:*

> High-purpose environments are filled with small, vivid signals designed to create a link between the present moment and a future ideal. They provide the two simple locators that every navigation process requires: *Here is where we are* and *Here is where we want to go.*[95]

Intentionally adding the identity dimension to a group or organization requires that you articulate your collective transcendent *why* and then consistently reinforce and measure it. Pearson's law states, "When performance is measured, performance improves. When performance is measured and reported back, the rate of improvement accelerates."[96] Studies show, for example, that the simple act of weighing yourself each day will help you lose weight, even with no other external action. If you take it to the next level and report your weight to a confidant each week, your level of improvement will further increase.

This same principle can be applied in a host of different areas where you want to see improvement.

In 2013, Andrew Howell and I started a law firm in Salt Lake City, Utah, with three attorneys, four staff members, and no plans to ever grow. Within the first five years, we had added a new named partner, Paxton Guymon, grown fivefold in size, and averaged sustained growth of 70 percent per year. Realizing we had become a large group of diverse individuals, we decided it was important to identify the shared values that would guide our firm as a collective whole. We ended up choosing four values that would mark how we wanted to be known:

- Connection—relating to another on a level where lasting bonds are made and meaningful community is created
- Artistry—honing the creative skills needed to take endeavors to a higher,
- more expressive level
- Generosity—giving of our time, effort, or resources (or even all three) without receiving back in a quid pro quo manner
- Excellence—striving for a high standard of quality even when doing so requires more effort, refusing to settle for mediocrity

While these may not be the four values that come to mind when you think of a stuffy law firm, they have infused the purpose and culture of our organization. The four primary conference rooms in our office space are named after these values. Employees can nominate their peers for our monthly CAGE award by recognizing one or more of these values in them. We have developed a set of questions, based on these values, that we regularly ask ourselves to see if we are on the right path. Even our annual reviews have been reformatted to identify and reinforce these values in how we work and relate to each other, to our clients, and to the community. These four values come together to create a North Star that guides us as an organization.

To start on the journey of discovering shared identity, again pick a group that you are a part of, and ask yourself the following:

1. Can my group articulate what we value and what we esteem?
2. Do we have a group identity, and if so, how would we describe it?
3. If we do have a group identity, is it the one we want?
4. What do we as a group aspire to be, and what difference do we want to make in the world?

## IMPACT

Finally, the fourth pillar of a steward-driven culture is impact, which flows from the very definition of a steward.

*Amount of Investment + Clarity of Purpose = Impact*

Here, the connection to investment and transcendence is obvious, and both parts of the equation are again critical. Groups that successfully develop stewards and that act as stewards themselves actively work toward meaningful goals and are able to articulate how they want to make a difference in the world. In fact, they view themselves as a team that has been assembled for that very purpose. While their ultimate aim may, like the dreams of Martin Luther King Jr. and others, be unattainable, that doesn't mean they don't set out to accomplish specific objectives that advance their aspirations and collectively move the ball forward.

When thinking about the difference you want to make as an individual or group, be careful not to fall for the false notion that impact is optional. It isn't. We all make one, for better or worse, whether we intend to or not. We should never attempt to opt out of making an impact or delude ourselves into thinking we won't have one on others. Eventually we all become the predecessors of the future. Saying you inherited a mess and complaining about the problems dumped on you by others is just a way of ducking responsibility. Those people who change the world invariably see themselves as preparing to *make* an impact, not merely to accept one. We may not have the final say on what our actual mark will be, but that doesn't mean we can't be intentional about the type of mark we strive to have on others.

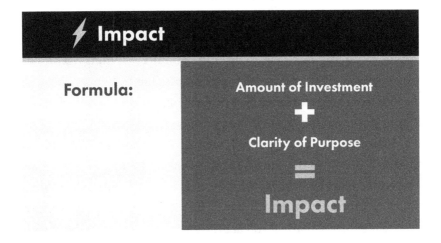

While knowing what kind of impact you want to make is a powerful tool for improving culture and efficacy, it can be a difficult tool to wield effectively, especially in the modern world. Perhaps the biggest obstacle in our quest for intentionality, either as groups or as individuals, is autopiloting, which occurs when we act on the basis of subconscious impulses, without deliberate or intentional thought.

Autopiloting begins early in life. When babies learn to walk, their brains are focused on every movement of the body, every undulation of the floor, every object around them they can use for support. As they become more accustomed to walking, however, those inputs are pushed to the subconscious so that more pressing matters can move to the forefront of their attention. While we may not remember the experience of learning to walk, we all remember learning to drive. We maneuvered slowly and deliberately, constantly checking our mirrors, our speedometer, our gauges, and other drivers, as we awkwardly attempted to navigate our parents' hulking vehicle down the street—and that was just to get to the neighborhood store. Years later, we find ourselves commuting mindlessly on overcrowded freeways and arriving at our destination wondering how we even got there. Sometimes we even arrive at the wrong destination because we were thinking about something else and autopiloted our way there.

A certain level of autopiloting is essential for life. By some estimates, the average person makes more than 35,000 decisions a day. If we didn't shift many of those decisions to the background (imagine having to consciously think about everything you do to simply walk), it would be virtually impossible to live any kind of productive life. Unfortunately, we don't consciously choose what our brains decide to move to the subconscious.

Psychologists Matthew Killingworth and Daniel Gilbert found that nearly half of the time—46.9 percent, to be exact—our brains are not actually focused on what we are doing.[97] While autopiloting allows us to function effectively in life, it comes with some major downsides, particularly if you are trying to be intentional about your purpose. First, because we don't actually choose what we move to the subconscious (this is done subconsciously), our brains may move things to the "reflexive action" bin that we should be staying more mindful of. Listening to others is a classic example of this. When someone is talking to us, our brains are often off making a grocery list or thinking about the latest episode of whatever show we've been binge-watching. But distracted listening is far from the only example.

Many times, we will react to something without even thinking about why we are doing so or noticing what feelings have been aroused. Much of the work done in counseling is simply an attempt to figure out what the brain is subconsciously up to when we react in ways we don't consciously understand. If we are not careful about what we're doing, we may consciously believe we are working toward a certain desired goal, and yet we may be behaving in a way that is counterproductive to that intended outcome.

The second problem with autopiloting is that it doesn't make us happy. Killingworth and Gilbert randomly interviewed more than 2,000 people at various times of their day to see what they were doing and how much thought they were putting into the task at hand. Participants were also asked to score their relative level of happiness while engaged in each activity. The researchers found that people were the happiest when having sex, exercising, and engaging in conversation. Those activities, uncoincidentally, also had the highest levels of mental engagement. The least happiness-inducing activities were resting, working, and using an electronic device, all of which also scored low on mental attentiveness. Unlike animals, whose minds are usually focused fully on the activities they are engaged in, we humans have the ability to perform an activity while mentally doing other things, such as reliving the past, thinking about the future, or daydreaming about the real or imagined. While that may make our brains unique, it doesn't make us happy. As Killingsworth and Gilbert determined, "A human mind is a wandering mind, and a wandering mind is an unhappy mind. The ability to think about what is not happening is a cognitive achievement that comes at an emotional cost."[98]

Meighan Sembrano reviewed this study (and others as well) and came up with six recommendations for reducing autopiloting and improving intentional impact.[99]

1.  **Focus on one task at a time.** The concept of multitasking has become ubiquitous in culture today. We think we are being more efficient if we are working while listening to a podcast on a treadmill and monitoring social media with some music in the background. Multitasking may be effective if you are performing some tasks that take little to no mental energy (like walking), but for things that require at least some level of attention, multitasking usually means doing multiple things poorly at the same time as opposed to one thing well.

2.  **Prayer or meditation.** Working on developing the art of prayer or meditation, the deliberate focus on the present

and on something bigger than yourself, can be difficult but can provide significant benefits. Often, meditation can have a spillover effect and allow you to concentrate during the day more easily.

3. **Kick off the stress.** While some level of stress can improve performance, prolonged levels of stress and the adrenaline it produces in the body can lead to increased rates of depression and decreased productivity and impact. Find activities you can engage in that not only make you feel less stressed (like exercise, being outside, engaging in conversation with a family member or friend) but can also help you improve focus and intentionality.

4. **Take short breaks and daydream.** While mind-wandering can have long-term negative impacts, there are some benefits to allowing the brain to go off on its own on occasion. Give your mind some freedom from time to time to wander off and dream. It fills the need that your brain has to go on the occasional walkabout and lets you scratch that creative itch, while also allowing you to be more present when not intentionally off in the clouds.

5. **Keep an eye on your thoughts.** Try and figure out what things you do or habits you have that lead to mind-wandering. If it's your phone (which for most of us it is!), consider turning off your notifications, or at least set it to silent mode during times that you want to be focused. Most computers and electronics allow you to put them into "Do Not Disturb" mode. Take advantage of that tool so you can concentrate and think.

6. **Improve your working memory.** Individuals with improved memory also have an increased ability to focus and report lower levels of mind-wandering. One study even found that people with higher working memory achieve their goals more quickly than those with lower memory. Consider employing some of the many tools and

resources available today that can help with improving memory.

Impact, the collective decision on how to express your group's shared identity, is critical to maintaining a healthy and positive culture because it ultimately pulls together the other pillars of communication, cohesion, and identity. It helps to create an environment of intentionality and focus and allows a group to avoid the pitfalls of inattention and the lack of joy that ensues when we fail to actively engage with our passions, ourselves, and others. That said, it can only be achieved when we are intentionally focused and are clear on how we want to impact our world.

Here are some questions regarding impact for your group:

1. Is your group's desired impact tied to its identity?
2. Does each person in your group know the specific impact you want to make?
3. Is each person meaningfully engaged in working toward the desired impact, or is that impact the vision of only one or a few members of the group?
4. Are there clear metrics for knowing whether or not your group is making the desired impact?

## Pillars of Culture

| Meaningful Investment | Transcendent Purpose | Pillar |
|---|---|---|
| Respectful Sharing | Respectful Listening | Communication |
| Engaged Relationship | Clarity of Purpose | Cohesion |
| Knowing Who You Are | Knowing Who You Want to Be | Identity |
| Amount of Investment | Clarity of Purpose | Impact |

CHAPTER 7

# Fostering Stewards

*"There are only two lasting bequests we can give*
*our children. One is roots, the other wings."*

**—Stephen Covey**

The fifty-two-word preamble to the United States Constitution is one of the most famous opening lines to any written document in American history. Its summation of the intent of the Constitution has served as the inspirational springboard for countless federal, state, and local laws. And when I say countless, I mean that literally. No one to date has been able to count all of the US laws currently in place, much less those previously enacted, although many people and organizations, including the Library of Congress, have tried.[100] The Internal Revenue Code, which only deals with federal tax law, contains over three million words alone and is 7,500 pages long.

The preamble itself seeks to lay out in simple terms exactly what the Constitution and, more broadly, our government, is all about. Its opening words are "We the People of the United States, in Order to form a more perfect Union." While certainly not without some debate as to its meaning, the phrase "more perfect Union" has generally come to signify our collective recognition that we, as a country, are not perfect but that we desire to strive toward that unreachable horizon in our words, ideals, and deeds.

No one would reasonably argue that the past or present state of our country could be described as anything approaching perfect. Slavery, racism, sexism, oppression, and intolerance have marked, and in many ways continue to mark, our nation. And yet, the United States has seen tremendous progress in many of these areas over the years. In 2008, then-presidential candidate Barack Obama gave a speech in Philadelphia, Pennsylvania, mere steps from where the Constitution was drafted. The speech became known as the "A More Perfect Union" speech, and, by most accounts, it was the most influential and important of his campaign. While primarily intended to address incendiary remarks made by his former pastor, much of Obama's speech focused on the desire to strive for an ever-better version of our nation. Obama acknowledged that we can become a more perfect union only when we acknowledge both our tremendous progress (which gives us hope) and our remaining problems (which provide us focus) and continue to push toward the ideals upon which the Constitution was written.

So, upon what principles or values should a nation be built? The theologian and philosopher Augustine of Hippo, in his treatise *The City of God*, defined a nation as a "multitude of rational beings, united by the common objects of their love."[101] Professor and author Jon Mecham expounded on this concept when he said that the ideal nation would have a common love of the following four things: equality of opportunity, justice before the law, supremacy of reason, and the efficacy of grace.[102]

In many respects, raising and developing stewards and building a "more perfect" family, organization, or community should embody these same elements. If we define families and groups as rational (or at least somewhat rational) beings united by the common objects of their love, then families or groups are in many ways like nations unto themselves, bound together by creed, purpose, and love. Families and groups that embrace the reality of where they are, and an understanding of where they want to go and who they want to be, have the greatest opportunity to foster and grow future stewards. Like a nation striving to be an ever-better embodiment of its ideals, tight-knit groups that encourage and embrace these elements of common love have the best chance to develop stewards and to advance their unique mission, vision, and values.

In the pages that follow, I'll delve into these four elements of common love and how they can be used to raise, develop, and foster stewards. I'll talk for the most part about families rather than nations, and parents rather than leaders, but I'll do so with the understanding that these four elements could work just as effectively for organizations, businesses, and religious or affinity groups.

| Four Key Building Blocks for Stewards | 1. *Equality of opportunity* |
| | 2. *Justice before the law* |
| | 3. *Supremacy of reason* |
| | 4. *The efficacy of grace* |

## EQUALITY OF OPPORTUNITY

In my work with families, I have learned that when it comes to wealth transfer, parents invariably strive to be two things above all others: fair and equal. When I started practicing law, I had the fanciful notion that these two terms were objective. I have since learned that they are two of the most subjective terms in the entire English language and that they invoke many different thoughts, feelings, and perspectives.

Parents who seek equality in their dealings with their wealth and their children can quickly become stymied when their children exhibit varying interests, needs, and life circumstances. Take, for example, the situation of a family with four children, two of whom are quite successful because of their hard work and some modest financial assistance from their parents, one of whom works a fulfilling job that pays little and struggles to care for her own family, and one of whom makes bad choice after bad choice. Two of the children really need no additional resourcing at all, one is in desperate need of assistance, and one might easily turn inherited resources into a furthering of self-destructive behavior. How should those parents allocate their resources among their children? What would be fair? Equal? "Fair" and "equal," as we can see, are far from simple terms.

For many, dealing with a family business in which some of the children are involved in the business and others are not can become another source of immense stress and family drama, especially when the family business represents a dominant portion of the family's overall wealth. Stress also arises when one or more of the children is facing a difficult circumstance that requires a disproportionate share of the parent's resources, and is exacerbated when the situation is fully or partially self-inflicted.

I once had a client who took equality to such an extreme that she kept a spreadsheet of every single Christmas gift she gave to children, grandchildren, and in-laws, noting the price paid for each item, and then wrote checks that equaled, to the penny, the difference between the highest amount given that year and the amount given to every other person.

As mentioned earlier in this book and in the book *Entrusted: Building a Legacy That Lasts*, the traditional model of estate planning typically follows the four-*D* model. This model involves *dumping* the assets on the next generation, *dividing* them equally among the children, attempting to *defer* any taxes, and *dissipating* those assets within one or two generations at most. This model *seeks* equality, but in the process obviates any cost associated with assets transferred and any investment on the part of the recipient. While well intentioned, a model that treats everyone equally in terms of distribution ends up undercutting the value of the wealth and is one of the primary reasons inherited wealth dissipates so quickly (i.e., eighteen months in the case of most Americans, and within one to two generations among even the wealthiest).

Instead of employing a traditional outcome-based model that seeks to divide assets equally, many high-net-worth individuals are beginning to pivot their planning, instead, toward an opportunity-based model that provides equal *opportunities*, though not necessarily equal distributions, to successive generations. This model can also be used by families with only modest resources. Rooted in the same desire for fairness and equality, the opportunity-based model recognizes that equality of opportunity is a higher form of fairness, one that allows cost and investment by the next generation to bring value to the family's resources. Such opportunity-based planning models can come in the form of encouragement and support for activities such as education, homeownership, charitable service, entrepreneurism, life enrichment, or other generationally engaging endeavors. When combined with the other elements of common love and the other principles outlined in this book, this model can often stop the erosion of wealth while also creating a structure that allows successive generations to build and grow their own wealth.

Regardless of the specific ways in which it seeks to support opportunities rather than mere consumption, this model can replace the four *D*s with the four *P*s: *purpose, perspective, preparation*, and *participation*. Two of the *P*s are based on transcendence, and two are based on investment. Taken together, they become the basis for creating an environment that fosters and develops opportunities and, in turn, stewards.

## PURPOSE

Purpose is the first and most important element of opportunity and, as we have seen before, is steeped in transcendence. There is no point in offering opportunities if you don't have an underlying purpose.

People who live engaged and impactful lives know who they are, what they value, and what they believe, and they know these same things about their family, employer, business, and community. As discussed throughout this book, the pull that comes from a transcendent purpose can help individuals take full advantage of the opportunities presented to them and encourage them to be fully invested. The greatest gift you can give a child, grandchild, employee, or community member is to help them foster their own sense of purpose. This can be accomplished by sitting down and going through the questions in chapter 5 with them and helping them understand and articulate what truly matters to them.

## PERSPECTIVE

The second opportunity-based element is perspective, and it is critical in the world today. By perspective, I mean the broadening of one's point of view. Perspective, like purpose, is based in transcendence and involves engaging in life beyond the self. Having a full spectrum of experiences, both in one's own community and around the world, can help a person better understand their own circumstances as well as the value of the opportunities that lie before them.

I once had a client who was planning a two-week vacation to a beach house in Hawaii that cost $25,000 a week and who worried that his children might get the wrong idea about what to expect from life in the present and the future. His solution was to make the kids fly coach while he and his wife flew first class. While perhaps nobly motivated, this exercise may not have given his children the perspective necessary to recognize the value of the opportunities they would likely enjoy in the future. Many of my other clients try to develop perspective in their children by spending time as a family while serving in their communities or working overseas in orphanages and other care organizations, having the children work demanding jobs with people in different socioeconomic circumstances, and/or encouraging travel to places other than five-star resorts.

## PREPARATION

The third element, and the first one that involves investment, is preparation, which entails providing meaningful education, tools, and resources to the children to help them understand how to manage and oversee their resources. A recent study that surveyed the children of high-net-worth individuals found that only 50 percent had engaged in even general conversations with their parents about wealth and money, only 19 percent had been offered financial literacy programs, only 12 percent had been taught about budgeting, only 10 percent had been taught about investments, and only 5 percent had been taught about the broader aspects of wealth.[103] These statistics are even more staggering when you realize they are culled from some of the most sophisticated and well-resourced families in the world.

Many children are asked to step into incredibly complicated business structures, plans, and investments without any meaningful preparation, education, or background. One client of mine struggled with the enormity of having his children take over the running of his more than fifty operating businesses. We decided that, instead of having them start as executives in the larger company, he would have each of them act as a comanager at one of his individual businesses and learn from the key employees and operators at that entity. By investing their time and talents in one business, they could not only learn critical skills and lessons but also follow the track of their father, who started with just one business himself.

## PARTICIPATION

The final element, which also relies on investment, is participation. It calls for the children to provide work and services as part of a family or business, to be given age-appropriate responsibilities, and to earn funds for their own needs.

Requiring participation from the children can often be a struggle, especially for higher-net-worth parents. Many of these individuals earned their wealth through hard work, stress, risk-taking, and sleepless nights. Surely the benefits of all that hard work should include making life easier for their children, right? While certainly understandable, this mindset can rob the children of the investment element that is critical for creating value in their lives. Another reason requiring participation can be a struggle is that it is actually more difficult for parents of means *not* to do something for their children than it is to force the children to do it for themselves. For these reasons, it is often harder—counterintuitively—to parent older children/young adults if you have too many financial resources than if you have too few. While there is nothing wrong with providing opportunities for your children, an element of personal participation should always be a part of any opportunity because, as previously stated in this book, we only value that which has a cost for us.

| Equality of Opportunity | | |
|---|---|---|
| | Purpose | Successful children know who they are, what they value, and what they believe and they understand those same things about their family. |
| | Participation | Successful children are actively participating in providing services as part of the family, have age-appropriate responsibilities, and earn funds for their needs. |
| | Preparation | Successful children are provided with meaningful education, tools, and resources to understand how to manage and oversee financial resources. |
| | Perspective | Successful children experience a full spectrum of life, both in their communities and around the World, and they understand that their circumstances are unique. |

## JUSTICE BEFORE THE LAW

Justice is a word not often used within families, and yet "injustice," or "unfairness," is often the cause of family divisions and broken relationships. Justice involves the fair and objective treatment of an individual within a system. It does not mean that the equal opportunities afforded to family members will result in an equality of outcome. Far from it. In fact, one of the things I always guarantee to families is that if they focus on providing equal opportunities to their children and grandchildren, different outcomes will invariably occur. These different outcomes will result from the children's life choices (educational, vocational, relational), their relationships (spouses, children, friends, coworkers, fellow investors), and their individual circumstances (health, tragedies, triumphs, successes, failures).

One of the most common ways *in*justice creeps into a family is through the parents' responses to these disparate outcomes. While I am certainly a strong supporter of parents' rights to use the resources they have accumulated in any way they see fit, the disproportionate application of those resources to try to *manufacture* equal outcomes among their children can often cause frustration, resentment, and embitterment.

So, how does a family balance its desire to treat its members justly with its goal of accomplishing two of the fundamental hallmarks of a strong team: meeting needs and caring for each other? First and foremost, any attempt at achieving justice within a family or organization should involve regular and healthy communication. While Lady Justice may be blindfolded, families should not be left in the dark. Family members should actively seek to communicate with each other and explain what they are doing and the principles upon which their major decisions are being made.

My wife and I had the "perfect" education plan for helping our children with college. And then our first child actually *went* to college. A hard worker, she nevertheless struggled initially in her classes, largely due to undiagnosed learning issues. These issues were eventually treated and allowed her to succeed. In the meantime, however, we had to learn how to balance the structure we had put in place against the principles we had built them on and the opportunities we were trying to encourage. As a result, we changed some of what we were doing and how we were doing it, but we communicated those changes to our daughter and also communicated to our other children how we would handle things for them moving forward.

Second, strategy and structure can be great tools for applying justice within any system. That said, strategy and structure should always be the caboose and not the engine. There is nothing wrong with having a good strategy and putting together a great structure, but both elements should flow from purpose. Often said another way in the business world, "Marry the vision. Date the strategy."[104] Clearly and concisely summarize the structure you want to put into place so you can fairly implement it, but also be willing to adjust your system as necessary to better effectuate your values, principles, and objectives. And, of course, communicate those changes to all concerned.

Many of my clients come to me with a desire to create a structure for minimizing their taxes, maximizing their return, protecting their assets, and controlling their resources. These are vitally important concerns, and need to be addressed, but in return, I ask these clients four questions (which you should ask yourself):

1. If you could transfer all your financial wealth without any tax or you could have grateful children, which would you pick?
2. If you could average a 12 percent return on your investments or you could have children who were self-reliant, productive, and mature, which would you pick?
3. If you could completely protect all your assets or you could have children who knew who they were and what they valued, which would you pick?

4.  If you could ensure that your assets were used exactly as you outlined or that your family members were engaged and connected with one another fifty years from now, which would you pick?

I'm not saying that control, asset protection, tax efficiency, and return on investment aren't important; they are, and they should be part of any effective plan. What I am saying is this: whenever I ask clients to prioritize between preparing their wealth for their children or preparing their children for their wealth, the resounding answer is that they want to prepare the children primarily. By focusing first on justice, fairness, and opportunity and then allowing those values to drive and direct your structure, you have the best opportunity for developing a plan that is purpose-driven and recipient-focused as opposed to structure-driven and asset-focused. A recipient-centered plan is far more likely to be positive and impactful.

## SUPREMACY OF REASON

Another word that isn't often applied within families is "reason"—not because families aren't reasonable (another topic for another book), but because, for most people, "family" is about "doing life" rather than planning rationally. As a result, too often we work—and even play—with a sense of reason and deliberative choice, but then rush home to make dinner, change diapers, clean the house, pay the bills, and mow the lawn. Reason, on the home front, is overwhelmed by the tyranny of the urgent. This leads to ambiguity in an area of our lives where clarity would be most beneficial. In too many families and organizations, purpose, roles, and responsibilities are undefined. In my experience, nothing hurts a family or organization more than uncertainty. Why? Because uncertainty inevitably leads to fear, worry, and self-preservation.

In her book *Rising Strong,* author Brené Brown makes the point that our brains are not designed for uncertainty. When we experience uncertainty, we make up a story to fill in the gaps, and that story *becomes* our reality unless and until it is replaced with actual reality. This is exacerbated in high-net-worth families, where there is often even greater uncertainty and a larger array of unknowns. In the study cited earlier in this chapter, only about 30 percent of children of high-net-worth individuals said that their parents had told them about how the family's wealth should be used, and only about 20 percent were provided with any information whatsoever on the structures for that wealth.[105] That means that the vast majority of heirs operate in a vacuum of knowledge when it comes to their family and its wealth.

The ambiguity caused by this lack of reason and explicitness leads to irrationality. Often the parents have not thought through the meaning and purpose of their own wealth and are living in ambiguity (and irrationality) themselves. In a study conducted by US Trust in 2017, a majority (54 percent) of high-net-worth individuals said their family would benefit from a formal set of values or principles to guide the handling of their wealth, but only 10 percent had actually implemented such a thing.[106] In another study, fully 90 percent of high-net-worth individuals said their estate plan did not advance their goals, values, and objectives.[107] In some cases, families are intentionally obtuse with the children regarding their wealth, hoping that a lack of communication will result in their children's assuming they should provide for themselves because their parents' plans are unknown (a strategy that rarely plays out as hoped).

I once had a client who shared with me, "My father told me that when I grew up, he wasn't going to leave me anything because he didn't have anything to leave, and that I had to go out and earn my own money. I believed him and worked really hard, so I've told my own kids the same thing."

In response, I said, "That's great. There's just one problem. You live in a seven-million-dollar house. They may not exactly buy what you're telling them."

For these reasons, I believe it is critical that every child, employee, partner, and colleague, in whatever group they belong to, be provided with the answers to three questions:

1. What can I expect being part of this family/ company/group?
2. What should I not expect?
3. What is expected of me?

**Three Critical Questions**

1. **What can I expect being part of this family/company/group?**
2. **What should I not expect?**
3. **What is expected of me?**

Of course, in order to provide answers to these questions, the parents or leaders must have thought through the questions themselves. This takes time and effort, but once accomplished (and communicated), it can result in tremendous peace of mind for both parents and children. Answering these questions is incredibly freeing because it not only allows both parent and child to move forward in life with clarity and understanding, it also sends an empowering message to the children that they can and will meet the expectations placed upon them.

## EFFICACY OF GRACE

Opportunity, justice, and reason are all powerful elements upon which to build any family or group, but it is the fourth element, grace, that can elevate these guiding principles and turn them into powerful love.

Grace, at its essence, is about offering to others what is unearned, undeserved, and perhaps unwarranted. In Mecham's summation of the elements of common love that a group or nation should embrace, the gift of grace becomes the counterbalance to the three other, more stoic elements, bringing life and wholeness to all of them.

There are three guidelines to remember as you infuse grace into your family. First, grace and truth must go hand in hand. Grace that is not accompanied by truth may in fact be indulgence or a lack of expectations. Grace without truth certainly cannot be considered love. When grace is employed—and it can be employed often—it should flow from clear-eyed wisdom and should never be used to lord the act of grace over someone or alternately excuse someone's lack of responsibility. Otherwise, grace comes across as violative of the other common loves of opportunity, justice, and reason, and can undermine each of them.

Second, grace should be seen as *completing* justice, not competing with it. In Victor Hugo's *Les Misérables*, Inspector Javert represents justice and reason. He spends his life consumed by hunting down Jean Valjean in order to bring him to justice for his perceived transgressions. For his part, Valjean, who has experienced many trials and inequities, responds to the life-changing grace he receives from a bishop by showing grace toward others. In the end, Javert is confronted with the knowledge that his brand of justice has been devoid of grace, and this knowledge leads him to an act of self-destruction. As you infuse grace into what you do, make sure it completes and encapsulates your values and transcendence.

Third, grace is relational and not transactional. It is all about giving and receiving benefits that have not been specifically earned. Grace should be expressed in a relationship and should bring freedom and blessing to both the giver and the recipient. If it doesn't do so, it is likely something other than grace—such as an attempt to help someone avoid consequences (which often means those consequences are borne by someone else). When a child heads off to college, for example, and leaves their room a mess, an act of grace might be to clean the room for them as an unmerited act of love that is embraced by the giver and appreciated by the recipient. If, on the other hand, the room is cleaned in anger and frustration (which would be the case if I were doing it), it's likely not grace, but rather an act born of frustrated duty or a selfish need to see the job done. If that's the case, it's probably better to let the other common loves win the day. This could be done by providing a sibling with the opportunity to clean the room at a generous price and then charging the absent child for that service. This response would be one that honors opportunity, reason, and justice.

Grace is the most impactful when it comes from the heart as well as the head.

| **Efficacy of Grace** | 1. Grace and truth must go hand in hand.<br>2. Grace should be seen as completing justice, not competing with it.<br>3. Grace is relational and not transactional. |
| --- | --- |

CHAPTER 8

# A Case Study in Un-Ownership

*"Once you have tasted flight, you will forever walk the earth
with your eyes turned skyward, for there you have been,
and there you will always long to return."*

**—Leonardo Da Vinci**

W hen John Montgomery decided to start his own financial
advisory company in 1993, he knew he wanted to do it
differently. Having grown up surrounded by affluence and seeing
the many problems and issues associated with having too much, he
knew that the primary focus of his new venture was not going to be
on maximizing profit. Rather, he specifically wanted to structure
his company, which he would eventually name Bridgeway Capital
Management, in response to the pitfalls of wealth and based on the
concepts of stewardship. He also knew that building a successful
financial advisory firm that wasn't founded primarily to achieve
financial success would take both planning and intentionality.

Inspired by a former boss who would take an entire year off before starting any new venture so that he had time to think and plan, John and his wife, Ann, took months developing a highly intentional mission statement and identifying the key elements of the business that would express the four core values outlined in that statement: integrity, performance, efficiency, and service.

The first decision that John and Ann made was to give away half the profits of the company each and every year. This decision was purposefully intended to minimize personal economic benefit and based on a desire to answer two critical questions:

1. Why would someone wait to give money away at the end of their lives when they could enjoy making a difference along the way?
2. What would it be like if a whole company was built around that idea?

While initially done in response to John's concerns about the dangers of excess, he quickly realized the power behind the principle. In fact, John credits this one decision as the single most powerful cause of Bridgeway's growth, and he believes that it has brought the company ten times more in total return than anything else he could have done with those profits. As John puts it, "Sometimes, I think if more businesspeople could get inside my head and see how powerful it is and how fun it is, corporate philanthropy would skyrocket."

Such an intentional focus on philanthropy had other benefits as well. It allowed Bridgeway to attract and retain like-minded people and has made operating the business infinitely easier because of that synergy. The generous nature built into the DNA of Bridgeway has attracted generous, others-centered people who are, by and large, far easier types of people to work with in a dynamic business. As John notes, "It's just so much easier to work at a business where everyone's values are aligned." It also makes decision-making so much easier because your values become a lens for viewing situations and charting a course for the future.

Beyond simply giving away half of the company's profits, Bridgeway also fundamentally views their people differently. In fact, Bridgeway doesn't have any "employees." Rather, everyone who works at Bridgeway is a "partner"—both in word and in practice. A portion of Bridgeway is owned by a PSOP, a partner stock ownership plan,[108] which provides retirement benefits to all of the company's partners. In another powerful signal that Bridgeway is different, they have also developed a unique compensation model that takes into account the compensation of everyone in the company from top to bottom. While many public and private companies could see disparities between the lowest and highest-paid employees of 400 times or more, Bridgeway has a much narrower band of compensation that they refer to as their stewardship commitment.

In practice, it means that there is significant financial "cost" among many of the higher compensated partners who could realistically make significantly more working somewhere else. That cost, however, as we see in the lives of so many stewards, means that there is actually more value placed on working at Bridgeway. Turnover at Bridgeway has been incredibly low, primarily because people who come to work at Bridgeway do so for more than just financial return, all without sacrificing talent level, ability, and success. Not only have the partners bought into the concept of generosity and impact, but they also tend not to be easily enticed away with promises of more money elsewhere.

This intentionality is more than lip service. Bridgeway is working toward being formally organized as a B Corporation, a special type of entity that can operate for reasons other than simply maximization of profit. B Corporations can legally alter the fiduciary responsibilities of the officers and directors of a business and allow them to consider the impact of their decisions on their workers, customers, suppliers, community, and the environment.[109] In addition, as a signatory to the United Nations Principles for Responsible Investment (UN PRI),

Bridgeway considers each of the following elements in their investment approach, known as ESG:[110]

- **Environment:** How a company mitigates its greenhouse gas emissions, whether the products the company creates are sustainable, if it uses natural resources efficiently, and how it deals with recycling.
- **Social:** The social component includes factors both inside and outside the company. Does the business participate in community development, such as providing affordable housing or fair lending? Does it carefully consider diversity and equal employment opportunity in its hiring? Does the company prioritize human rights everywhere it does business, including other countries?
- **Governance:** Governance (or corporate governance) refers to the company's leadership and board, including whether executive pay is reasonable, if the company's board of directors is diverse, and whether it's responsive to shareholders.

Perhaps the most unique and fascinating element of the Bridgeway story is its principal philanthropic endeavor. Although the company gives to a variety of different charitable organizations and initiatives of interest to its partners, the primary focus has been on the elimination of genocide in the world. This work is done by and through the Bridgeway Foundation and its CEO Shannon Sedgwick Davis, who details some of this work in her gripping book *To Stop A Warlord*.

While attempting to eradicate genocide may seem like a bit of a non sequitur for the founder of a financial advisory firm, it is one that is deeply personal to John. As a teenager, John took a US history class and studied World War II, a war in which his father had fought. Prior to that class, John had never heard of the words *genocide* or *holocaust*, and he remembers having a visceral reaction to both. The concept of trying to eradicate a people group simply because of their race or religion was just so beyond the pale to him. It was then that he began to foster a powerful desire to protect the vulnerable and bring peace to those suffering persecution and abuse. This desire to change the world ultimately led John and Ann to start a company whose profits could be used for such an end, and it's what inspires them and those who work with them to bring success to both.

When it comes to the future of Bridgeway, that is something that John and Ann have been highly intentional about as well. They recently established a *purpose trust*, which is a special type of trust designed not to benefit specific individuals but rather to achieve certain specific purposes. Purpose trusts have become more common over the past twenty to thirty years, which makes them fairly recent creations, considering the origins of common law trusts go back more than 1,000 years. That said, an increasing number of jurisdictions are adopting or updating their purpose trust statutes to allow for greater flexibility when it comes to establishing these special kinds of trusts so that broader purposes and objectives, many of which combine social, civic, and philanthropic goals, can be achieved. In fact, in 2019, Oregon became the first state to pass a stewardship trust statute, which allows for purpose trusts to hold business assets (and literally steward assets) for potentially multiple generations. For purpose trusts to be valid and enforceable, they must clearly articulate their purpose and must have actual "enforcers" who can ensure that the trust is operated by its trustees to effectuate those objectives.

For their part, John and Ann have begun transferring some of their interest in the company to the purpose trust, and ultimately the plan is for the purpose trust to be the primary shareholder of Bridgeway. The trustees of the purpose trust will work to ensure the current and future partners of Bridgeway Capital Management can be successful and continue to support and finance charitable initiatives like Bridgeway Foundation. Part of this is from John and Ann's desire to see Bridgeway continue to do well so that it can continue to do *good*. It's also the result of them realizing that stewardship means that you are only entrusted with something for a period of time, and that if you want to make a lasting impact, you need to not only focus on your current success but also on your future successors.

CHAPTER 9

# Pulling It All Together

*"You haven't seen a tree until you've seen its*
*shadow from the sky."*

**—Amelia Earhart**

O ne of the most tragic myths of the Western world is that
meaning and impact can be achieved only by those who possess
considerable personal resources or natural ability. Too often we
sideline ourselves because we believe that others who have "more"
can accomplish more than we ever could. We think that because
they can do something we can't or because they own something we
don't, they are destined to be the gladiators in the ring, and we are
destined to be the spectators in the crowd.

The truth is, such false notions enable us to avoid the responsibility
that comes with conviction. The real reason stewards are so impactful
in our world is that they truly possess only two things: a compass and
a pair of boots. Their compass informs them of where they are and
where they want to go. Their boots allow them to move into action in
the direction in which their compass points and to demonstrate their

belief in their chosen course to themselves and others. Stewards, as we have seen, are not "ordained" based on gender, race, creed, religion, or economic status. They are found in every part of our world, in every stratum of culture and economy. The quality that identifies them as stewards is their complete devotion to something bigger than themselves.

Throughout this book we have cited examples of stewards, including the likes of Lucius Quinctius Cincinnatus, George Washington, Nelson Mandela, Martin Luther King Jr., Susan B. Anthony, and Jesus of Nazareth. With a list like that, it would be easy to become overwhelmed by the prospect of becoming a steward. You might be inclined to ask, "Without the resources of a multimillionaire, the power of a high-level politician, or the convictions of a world leader, how could *I* possibly make an impact as a steward?"

To show that stewards can come from any walk of life and from little to no material wealth, I want to end with a story that has been too seldom told. It is the account of the roughly 12,000 conscientious objectors (COs) during World War II who formed the Civilian Public Service (the CPS).[111]

Of the more than thirty-four million men who signed up for the United States draft in the 1940s, about 77,000 of them refused, for mostly religious reasons, to serve in combat roles. About one-third of them ended up in noncombat roles in the Army, with perhaps the most famous of these being Desmond Doss, whose story was captured in the movie *Hacksaw Ridge.* Another one-third of them failed the medical examinations and weren't required to serve. Of the rest, many chose service in the CPS, which had been established by the US federal government in collaboration with the leaders of the religious denominations that most ardently opposed the violence of warfare—namely, the Mennonites, the Religious Society of Friends (the Quakers), and the Church of the Brethren. In exchange for avoiding either conscription in the Army or imprisonment, these men assumed roles of critical national importance. Because so many able-bodied men had joined the military, the CPS enlistees took on many difficult and dangerous civilian vocations, all for little to no pay, supported financially by their local congregations. Many women joined the cause as well.

Some of the COs took jobs as forest firefighters, while others worked on soil erosion projects and on dairy farms. Many were assigned to understaffed mental health institutions throughout the United States, where they often encountered horrific conditions. The COs worked hard to improve conditions for the patients and brought much-needed attention to the situation. Eleanor Roosevelt, who was initially skeptical of the merit of the CPS, not only came around to supporting it but also championed the cause for better patient treatment and rallied many other well-known names of the day to the cause.[112] Major mental health reforms resulted from the advocacy of the CPS workers in those facilities.

Within the ranks of the CPS, a group of about 500 men even volunteered to serve as human guinea pigs for medical experimentation. These experiments, which would never be condoned today, were carried out to help researchers learn how to more effectively treat soldiers and civilians who had been subject to the horrors of war. Some of the participants were intentionally infected with hepatitis to test the efficacy of various treatments. Others were exposed to lice, which transmitted typhus and cholera, and then treated with DDT to determine the effectiveness of the chemical and to study any side effects. And others were subject to either exposure or prolonged dehydration, including one group that was kept in a frigid room while wearing soaking-wet clothes to study what types of fabrics would be the best for soldiers.

From among the ranks of the COs, thirty-six men agreed to participate in a long-term starvation program, the objective of which was to develop the best practices for reintroducing sustenance to the severely malnourished. Responding to a pamphlet titled "Will You Starve That They Be Better Fed?", those who volunteered underwent a three-phase experiment.[113] The first phase involved twelve weeks of medical testing and diagnostics in which virtually every part of their body was subject to analysis and measurement. That was followed by nearly six months of starvation, where their calories were restricted to the point that they lost, on average, 25 percent of their body weight. In the third phase, they were divided into different groups and slowly reintroduced to food, all in an effort to see which approach was most effective. The results were ultimately published by the University of Minnesota in the two-volume *The Biology of Human Starvation.*

During the course of the experiment, participants faced many hardships. They experienced severe fatigue, dizziness, muscle soreness, hair loss, and ringing in their ears. They became so fatigued that many needed help opening doors or even lifting their feet to step up on a curb. Beyond the physical effects of starvation, the psychological effects were also studied. Subjects of the experiment became obsessed with food. One participant became so fixated on cookbooks that he amassed a collection of more than a hundred by the end of the experiment. Another recalled walking by a bakery and becoming so entranced by the smell that he rushed into the bakery and purchased a dozen donuts, only to hand them out to passersby so he could watch them eat. Others could not bear to watch anyone eat or would add water to their meager rations to make them appear bulkier.

What may be the most remarkable aspect of the Minnesota Starvation Experiment, as it came to be called, was the resolve and determination of the participants. They not only willingly volunteered to starve but they willed themselves through the entire process. Of the thirty-six participants, only one could not endure the starvation and left the program. The rest saw it as their way to sacrifice themselves in a similar way to those who had gone to war. While their convictions called for them to refuse to take the life of another, those same convictions impelled them to lay down their own lives for others. Participant Marshall Sutton expressed it this way: "Our friends and colleagues in other places were putting their lives on the line, and you know, we wanted to do the same." As framed by another participant, Samuel Legg, "Everyone else around us is pulling down the world; we want to build it up."

These experiments, which most would condemn today, helped advance the care and treatment of millions around the world. The researchers learned critical methods for bringing people back from starvation and malnutrition, as well as how to effectively treat many other ailments and health issues. The experiments also led to advances in the fight against hepatitis, malaria, and typhus.

The men of the CPS had no material resources and were not selected because of any innate skills or abilities. Rather, they were mere pacifists who were asked to serve in the midst of a war that was ravaging the planet. Even so, they left an indelible mark on not only their country but also the rest of the world. Their sacrifices were born out of their transcendent beliefs—in nonviolence and in loving and caring for others—which led to their complete personal investment.

## CONCLUSION

The path of the steward is both challenging and rewarding, both deeply personal and outwardly expressive. Born from an insatiable desire for the best, it asks for personal sacrifice but ultimately leads those who follow it to freedom. Those who embrace the way of the steward not only find the peace that comes from counterbalancing transcendence and investment, they also leave an indelible mark on the lives of their friends, families, and communities—and on the world itself.

APPENDIX

# Stewards and
# the Family Business

R ivers have always played an important role in human history.
Often serving to bring power, resources, and prominence to a
location, they serve as a means of transportation, provide sustenance
and enjoyment, and create natural borders for cities, states, and
nations around the globe.

Some rivers twist and flow on a solitary path before meeting
another river, the junction of which is known as a confluence. A
confluence can inherit several new characteristics the individual rivers
did not possess, such as rough waters, changes in color, and differences
in the speed of water flow. They can even produce an entirely new
biological makeup. There are many picturesque confluences in the
world that serve as stunning examples of what can happen when rivers
merge. One such scene is in Passau, Germany, where the Danube, Ilz,
and Inn Rivers form a confluence that has three distinct stripes, each
a different shade of blue or green.

Family businesses often resemble the confluence of two rivers.
The family unit can be thought of as one river, the business as another.

Both are distinct and have their own characteristics, but together they can create a beautiful and unique melding. Just as with joining rivers, though, the confluence of a family and a business can be turbulent. It can create rough, choppy waters that make navigation difficult. Over time, however, the rivers adjust to the flow, and, little by little, the rocky terrain beneath the water can be smoothed. The hardships and growing pains the family may experience in the early days of running a business can eventually calm and produce a beautiful confluence like those in nature. When the family members lean on one another for support during the challenging start-up period, the waters can calm even faster.

One of the most powerful ways stewards can make a positive impact in the world is within a family business. By harnessing their own confluence of transcendence and investment, they can help to bring vision, stability, and purpose to family businesses, which in turn can lead to long-term viability. By their very nature and temperament, stewards are the ideal overseers of family businesses because they bring transcendence to their organizations, as well as deep investment and engagement. Before delving into how stewards can make such positive impacts, it is important first to understand the unique aspects of family businesses as well as the challenges they face.

## FAMILY BUSINESSES ARE UNIQUE AND POWERFUL

A family business is defined as a business actively owned or managed (or both) by more than one member of the same family. When the average person thinks of a family business, they envision a mom-and-pop outfit, such as a small grocery store, a bakery, a boutique shop, or other such modest enterprises. The reality is that family businesses are dominant players in the national and global market. Giants such as Walmart, Mars, Comcast, Ford, and Motorola are family-owned and operated. One third of companies in the S&P 500 index are defined as family businesses, and the top ten family businesses generated $1.3 trillion in revenue and employed more than 3.6 million people in 2017.

Family businesses are the single biggest job creator in our economy, employing over 60 percent of the US workforce. They are responsible for 78 percent of all new jobs created in the US, and they generate a whopping 64 percent of the gross domestic product.[114] Family-owned or controlled businesses make up 90 percent of American businesses.[115] The message is clear: family businesses are a crucial part of the American marketplace, and with dedication and hard work, a well-conceived family business can look forward to becoming a successful enterprise.

There are numerous reasons why family businesses are positioned to thrive. For example, family businesses enjoy the benefits of captive capital. Publicly traded companies and non-family businesses typically seek outside capital or debt to build and grow their enterprises and must grapple with the demands of shareholders and creditors as well as the visions of CEOs, who are far too often more interested in bottom lines than culture. Family businesses, on the other hand, have the advantage of investing their own money and resources, which allows them to foster longevity and promote the desired culture of the business.

By contrast, a 2005 survey conducted by the *Journal of Accounting and Economics* found that 78 percent of CFOs of publicly traded companies admitted they would be willing to make decisions that destroy value over the long term in order to achieve their quarterly earnings target. C-suite executives of publicly traded companies certainly understand the value of the more closely held model; 84 percent of CEOs stated it would be easier to manage their company if it were private.[116]

While it might be tempting to believe that the trade-offs made by public companies result in greater profit margins, that is not necessarily true. Family businesses, on average, enjoy greater returns on investment than S&P 500 companies.[117]

An additional asset of a family business is its ability to maintain a stellar workplace culture. By nature, family businesses tend to be more people-oriented, and their company values are often stronger than those of publicly traded companies, with 74 percent of family businesses reporting the conviction that they have stronger cultures and values than non-family firms.[118] Family businesses are less likely to lay off employees, even when facing difficult times financially, and have 20 percent less annual turnover than non-family businesses.[119] The reason for this cultural strength is simple: family businesses enjoy strong support networks that stem directly from family members who have an inherent sense of cohesion and identity. Values and ethics shared among family members are reported as being the most important advantages of the family-business model.[120]

In addition to their strong monetary performance and cultural values, family businesses also have an advantage in longevity. Family business models tend to adopt more long-term-oriented strategies than their non-family counterparts. Family businesses prefer to use excess cash flow to finance their investment projects rather than to distribute them as dividends to family shareholders on a short-term basis.[121] The more the family is in control of the business, the lower the amount of dividend distribution to shareholders.[122]

As a result of their prudent choices, family businesses tend to be less indebted than non-family businesses, which tends to make them much more likely to survive trying economic situations.[123] A study conducted by the Management Research Center at Ecole Polytechnique compared 149 family-controlled businesses with similarly sized non-family businesses. The results showed that while family businesses slightly underperform non-family businesses in good economic times (14 percent growth versus 12 percent growth), family businesses significantly *outperform* their counterparts during tough economic times (11 percent versus 4 percent growth) in all seven countries the researchers studied (the United States, Canada, France, Spain, Portugal, Italy, and Mexico). The study also found that family businesses' investment of their own capital, which made them less susceptible to the demands of outside creditors and investors, and their ability to attract and retain good employees were two of the main reasons for this dramatic difference.

## FAMILY BUSINESSES FACE SIGNIFICANT RISKS

While there are many positive aspects of family businesses, there are perhaps just as many risks and potential pitfalls.

First, family businesses tend to avoid certain issues that non-family businesses more often address, especially when it comes to succession planning. Only 16 percent of family firms have discussed and documented such plans.[124] Even more surprising, 47 percent of family business owners who anticipate retiring within the next five years do not have successors.[125] Although 70 percent of family businesses want the business to be passed to the next generation, only 30 percent succeed in accomplishing this goal. The statistics dwindle from there. Only 10 percent make it to the third generation and barely 5 percent make it to the fourth.[126]

Family business owners are largely unaware of these risks. In one study, business owners were asked about what factors concerned them as they looked to the future. Only 7 percent of those surveyed stated it would be family dynamics and relationships, while 41 percent speculated it would be estate and financial planning risks, 36 percent envisioned economy, business, and financial market risks as the culprits, and 16 percent believed political and tax risks would be their greatest challenges.[127] These fears, however, are at odds with experienced reality. When those same researchers asked businesses that had faced significant transitional struggles about what *actually* harmed their business, a mere 3 percent of family business owners reported failures in financial and estate planning, taxes, and investments. Of the rest, 37 percent responded that the harm was due to unprepared successors, and an astonishing 60 percent cited lack of communication and trust in family members as the cause.[128] The very thing business owners thought was the least of their worries ended up causing the greatest amount of harm to their businesses' ongoing success.

Research shows that an honest discussion about family and business values, a solid succession plan, and clear expectations about the future of the family business are key to long-term success. Without these elements, an otherwise promising family business can be quickly and permanently torn apart. As I counsel many of my clients, I find that family businesses typically fail to successfully transition for two primary reasons. Either they remember it's a business but forget it's a family, or they remember it's a family and forget it's a business. Typically, only family businesses that understand and balance both of these elements are able to survive and thrive.

## THE SIX TYPES OF FAMILY BUSINESSES

Before a succession plan can be adopted, the current family business model should be identified and understood. There are six unique types of family businesses, each with their own distinguishable traits and risks. In assessing which model a family business fits into, the critical question is not *What type of family business does the family have?* but rather *What kind of family business does the family* think *it has?* Understanding family perceptions of the business is critical for those enterprises that want to have a sustainable long-term model. The family member who is most invested in the business may have a completely different view of the family business dynamic than her family members and coworkers. For that reason, understanding one another's point of view can help guide the business leaders to make beneficial changes to the business structure.

1. **The Siloed Family Business:** In this type of business, the lines between family and business are stark and

uncrossed. The family wears their business-only hats at the factory and their family-only hats at the dinner table. The siloed family business is rare and difficult to maintain. Very few families can devote significant time and resources to the business only to return home at the end of the workday and talk about nothing but sports, politics, and the weather.

2. **The Overlapping Family Business:** The overlapping family business is much more common than the siloed model. These family businesses attempt to keep home and business matters separate, with the understanding that the two will naturally intersect sometimes. For example, the family may discuss upcoming work schedules over dinner, bring up new ideas for the business in casual conversation, and/or attend seminars or other business-related activities together during their leisure time. That said, for the most part, they keep business and family separate, with only modest levels of bleed between the two.

3. **The Overreaching Family Business:** This model is one in which the lines between family and business regularly become blurred. An example of this model can be seen in TLC's hit television series *Cake Boss.* The patriarch of the family, Buddy Valastro, runs the business (a successful bakery), and many other immediate and extended family members work for the bakery in various capacities. Those who don't work for the business often assist from time to time on big projects or during busy seasons. Though some members of the family do not work in the shop, and though the family members make it a point to enjoy time together outside of work, the bakery is often the focus of conversation at the home dinner table. Likewise, family matters are often discussed in the commercial kitchen.

4. **The "Business Is Family and Family Is Business" Family Business:** In this model, there is no separation between the family and the business. The two are completely intertwined, and a conversation or activity focused on business may easily transition to the topic of family and vice versa. The breakfast table can become the boardroom in an instant. This model can easily arise when a family is running a busy home-based business, such as a dispatching service, or when they live at or very near their place of work. Imagine a family that owns a hotel and lives in one of the suites. The food they eat is prepared by the hotel, the hotel staff does their laundry and cleans their living areas, and they spend the majority of their free time at their place of business. In such a situation, it becomes difficult, if not impossible, to distinguish home life from business.

5. **The His, Hers, and Ours Family Business:** While this type of business can resemble any of the previous four examples, it is unique in the sense that not all family members are involved in the operation of the business. A family business model of this type might occur, for example, in a professional services company. In a family of, say, five, if three of the family members are lawyers and decide to open a firm together, the remaining two non-lawyers would likely not participate in the family business. The Venn diagram of this family would show three circles with some members overlapping between the two spheres and others remaining separate.

6. **The In-and-Out Family Business:** In this case, the family members who are part of the business feel included, but those who are not part of the business feel isolated, almost as if they are not part of the family. This type of family business model can occur when a child desires to do something other than be a part of the family business.

If the family runs a successful restaurant, for example, and the eldest child decides she would like to join the medical field after graduation, this might cause a rift between the daughter and the other family members. This dynamic can also happen in some of the other models; the family members don't know how to relate to one another outside of the construct of the business.

## THE FOUR TYPES OF FAMILY-BUSINESS SUCCESSORS

Just as there are different types of family businesses, there are also different types of potential successors. One of the most critical aspects of family business continuity is having a clear plan for succession. Selecting the right successor is crucial. In order to make the right choice in succession, the family business owner should understand the four types of business successors and consider their strengths and weaknesses in light of how they can best serve the future of the business. Here we revisit the four character types we explored in chapters 2 and 3.

- **Consumers.** The most common type of successor in a family business is, unfortunately, the consumer. Consumers are those who live in the moment and fail to focus on the long-term goals and visions of the family business. While they don't invest much time, talent, or treasure in the business, they feel entitled to reap the business's benefits due simply to their status as a member of the family. This consumer mindset is a main reason that the average lifespan of an inheritance is only eighteen months and that only 30 percent of family businesses make it into the next generation.
- **Dreamers.** Dreamers are less common in a family business. While they may have great hopes for the business and may

even understand its unique culture and potential impact on the world, they don't invest personally in the business. This is typically because they lack the willingness or ability to invest, although, tragically, sometimes it is simply because they were never asked to invest. It may also be that their hopes and dreams are largely disconnected from (or unable to be expressed within) the family business.

- **Owners.** An owner is an individual who will take charge immediately and build the business. They are all in, all the time. While their impact can be significant, owners are not necessarily interested in maintaining the business for the long term. Rather, they often hope to make the business more profitable or valuable, and then transfer its ownership and move on to the next project once they have regained their investment plus some.

- **Stewards.** The steward is the type of successor most family business owners hope for. Stewards dedicate themselves fully to the family business and its purpose. They transcend mere ownership of the business, and, as a result, they can make long-term decisions that look to purpose and not merely profits. They make a profound difference and remain loyal to the purpose of the business, which includes having an impact not only on the bottom line but also on the business's employees, customers, and communities. Because of the long-term mindset of stewards, they are unthreatened by the thought of successors. In fact, they embrace and encourage future leaders and long-term planning for the business.

## HOW TO BUILD A SUCCESSION PLAN

Once the business model and successor type are identified, the family business owner must decide the best course of action for succession.

Considering the traits of each type of successor, the following recommendations are likely to be in the best interest of both the family and the business.

For those who have consumers as successors, the best choice is probably to sell the business. Too often, the lack of personal investment and connection to the *why* of the business will result in a diminution of value for the business or even its demise. For family businesses that see this coming, they might sell the business before the consumer takes over and while the business is still at it highest value. Otherwise, the sale may happen after the consumer takes over and the business has begun to falter.

If the successors are dreamers, there are two potential options. The first option applies in the case where the successor might simply be a dreamer because they haven't been *asked* to invest. The parents, in this case, may have sacrificed a great deal to build the business and were hoping to spare their children such hardship, not realizing that the heavy cost associated with building the business was what helped bring value to it. In such situations, requiring a dreamer to make a substantial personal investment of time, talent, or treasure may actually help propel them to become a steward.

The other option applies if the dreamer simply does not have the skill sets to effectively operate the business. Here, a bifurcated approach might be used. Rather than entrust a dreamer with the whole business, it might make sense to put them in charge of, say, the culture and purpose of the business, and retain other key employees to handle the day-to-day tasks of the business. One-quarter of businesses that plan on transitioning their business to the next generation enlist outside management to oversee the key operational and financial aspects of running the company.[129] There is no harm in joining this sizable minority if it will be in the best overall interest of both the business and the family.

For those with owners in their succession line, consider either selling them the business or at least putting a buy-sell agreement in place so they will ultimately be able to acquire the business. While some will sell their business to owner-successors on more favorable terms than the market's, many realize the benefits of an arm's-length transaction so that their successors truly know and appreciate the value they are acquiring. If a purchase is likely to occur down the road, sometimes it might make sense to lock in a price based on today's value. That way, the owner-successor can try to grow the business's value without feeling that they are ultimately working against him or herself. Regardless of how they acquire the business, owner-successors will in all likelihood treat the handoff as a business transaction and make good decisions about the future of the business.

For those lucky enough to be graced with stewards as successors, the succession plan should begin as early as possible. Stewards should be introduced to the business at an early age so they can be educated, purposed, and equipped to take over with ease once the time comes. In the meantime, continue to help them understand both their personal transcendence and the purpose and vision of the business while you simultaneously work to foster investment on their part. This could include allowing them to spend time working in all aspects of the business, supporting the development of their personal skills and talents, and allowing them to earn their own financial resources and invest them into the business.

Rarely do all potential successors fit neatly into one of these boxes. Usually, families have a combination of all of these types. If so, the family business must decide whether it would like to be governed by the least common denominator (the consumer) or do the harder work of creating an individually tailored plan that takes into account each of the different types of successors. If this family business fails to focus on providing equal *opportunity* for all, and instead falls into the trap of giving all potential successors equal power or ownership, the outcome will invariably be less desirable than if it divides the roles and responsibilities between the different successors according to their strengths. Another factor that must be considered is each successor's ability to contribute to the business and their personal interest level in doing so. The family business must look at fair compensation and ownership for each of the successors and make the choice that will be most beneficial for the business.

## BUILDING BLOCKS OF STEWARDSHIP: PURPOSE AND CULTURE

Stewards who seek to eventually operate the family business should, as outlined previously in this book, spend significant time and resources focusing on purpose and culture.

**Purpose.** Purpose is the reason for which an organization exists. It is the overall goal or aim of a family business. Having a clearly defined purpose improves morale and profit alike. Employees who are inspired by the company for which they work are more satisfied, more productive, and less likely to think about leaving.[130] Consider the following:

The University of Michigan operated a call center wherein students contacted alumni of the university, seeking donations for scholarships. The rejection rate for donations was 93 percent. The call center leaders put a plan of purpose into action and began inviting scholarship recipients to come to the call center for five minutes and share two things with the student volunteers: where they came from and what the money raised meant to them. After this practice was implemented, the time students spent calling alumni increased by 142 percent, and weekly revenues increased by 172 percent.[131] The best part? This shift of focus cost the company nothing, and no changes needed to be made to the structure or operations of the company. The only thing that changed was the infusion of purpose.

How can purpose be enhanced in a business? When leaders are perceived as mentors and strong advocates for employee development, the odds of employees feeling that their organization and work have purpose increase by 433 percent, and the odds of employees being engaged in their work increase by 837 percent.

**Culture.** Culture, as mentioned in chapter 6, is defined as the attitudes and behavioral characteristics of an identified group. Cultural norms prescribe what is encouraged, discouraged, accepted, or rejected within a group. As noted earlier, there are four attributes of culture: (a) it is shared within a group, (b) it permeates multiple levels of an organization or society and applies very broadly, (c) it endures beyond the comings and goings of any specific individuals, and (d) while it is subliminal, people are hardwired to recognize and respond to it instinctively. The strength of a company's culture, as defined by the degree of agreement on cultural characteristics, correlates with financial performance.[132] The stronger the culture, the more profitable the company.

Family business owners can follow four steps to create a positive and lasting culture for their business. First, they should articulate the aspiration. This involves understanding the current culture and identifying the type of culture that is in the business's best interest. Second, leaders should exemplify the desired culture. The hiring of new managers and leaders should focus on whether or not the candidates align with the target culture of the business. Third, leaders should discuss culture with their employees and ensure they understand the importance of making change that promotes the desired culture and know the steps necessary to achieve such change. Fourth, the leaders should reinforce the desired changes via organizational design. All processes should support the desired culture and strategy of the business. Change cannot take root if it is implemented only at the top; it must be cultivated from the ground up.

## STEPS TOWARD SUCCESSION

Once the family business has established a strong culture and purpose, the emphasis needs to shift toward developing stewards to take over the business. Stewards should focus on culture over strategy, be adequately compensated, be given age-appropriate responsibilities, and be held accountable for their actions toward the family business, whether positive or negative. The family business leaders should work toward instilling a sense of belonging, purpose, and transcendence throughout their business, and should pass those elements along to the steward.

Family businesses can achieve a culture of *belonging* by building relationships of mutual care and by orchestrating frequent pleasant interactions with staff. In some businesses, employees can work for years in an office or on a warehouse floor without even meeting a member of upper management, let alone having a pleasant interaction with one. These employees feel easily replaceable and dissociated from the business.

*Purpose*, as discussed earlier, can be instilled by establishing a clear and far-reaching goal that is understood by all members of the family business.

*Transcendence* can be achieved by understanding how the business contributes to the world. Whether the family business is a small convenience store or a large multistate retailer, it must understand how it fits into the community at large and how it affects the population it serves.

*Story* is the vehicle by which all of these elements are communicated to team members and brought to life. Human beings, by nature, tend to seek the story behind a company or group before investing loyalty in it. The family business should take every opportunity to share its story, not only with present-day staff members but also with the business's successors, in order to achieve a true buy-in from future generations. In a very real sense, it is the *story* of the business that the steward nurtures and carries forward into the future.[133]

# Transcendent Questions

*What is the greatest compliment I could ever receive? That I could ever give?*

*What virtues bring tears to my eyes when I see them embodied? Why?*

*Whom do I admire the most, and what is it about him or her that I admire?*

*What does the world need now more than ever?*

*What is one of the best ways to express love?*

*What part of my story am I most proud of?*

*What gets me excited in life?*

*When and where am I the most myself?*

*Who are my others?*

*How does what I love positively affect the lives of others?*

*If what you love doesn't impact others, is it worth loving?*

*What is the good life?*

*What is the good man? The good woman?*

*What is the good society, and what is my relation to it?*

*What are my obligations to society?*

*What is best for my children?*

*What is justice? Truth? Virtue?*

*What is my relationship to nature?*

*What is my relationship to death, aging, pain, and illness?*

*How can I live a zestful, enjoyable, meaningful life?*

*Who are my brothers and sisters and what is my relationship to them?*

*What shall I be loyal to?*

*What must I be ready to die for?*

*What do I love?*

*For each thing I love, why do I love it?*

*Is it something temporary?*

*Is it a person? If so, do I love who that person is or how they make me feel?*

*Is there anything transcendent about what I love?*

*Is what I love bigger than myself or simply something I can buy, experience, or consume?*

*What loves of mine take precedence over other loves?*

*What loves should move up my list?*

*What loves should move down my list or be taken off altogether?*

*Is there something behind what I think I love that is actually capturing my heart?*

*Am I trying to value too many things?*

*Which of my values should rise to the top?*

*If I could be known for only three things, what would I want them to be?*

*Is my transcendence actionable (i.e., can I do something to advance its cause)?*

*What am I looking for?*

*Who am I looking for?*

*Why am I afraid?*

*Where is my faith?*

*Why do I doubt?*

This is my transcendence:

_____

_____

_____

_____

_____

_____

_____

_____

_____

_____

_____

_____

_____

_____

_____

_____

_____

_____

_____

_____

_____

_____

_____

_____

_____

_____

_____

_____

_____

*If I had extra time, this is how I would spend it:*

_____

_____

_____

_____

_____

*This is the talent I will invest in improving or developing:*

_____

_____

_____

_____

_____

*This is how I will invest any additional resources:*

_____

_____

_____

_____

_____

# My Transcendence

I believe that I was created by God. If I was created, then I have a purpose. I believe that purpose is to love God, the One who created me. He wants me to love Him because He wants the best for me, and He is that best. The best way to love God is to love His other creations and to do so in the way that I was made. I value thinking, creating, relating, giving, and moving. As a result, I will try and love others through doing the following:

*Think*—I love ideas, especially ideas that change the world and improve the lives of others. I will seek out new ideas, put old ideas together in new ways, and generously share my thoughts and ideas with others so that they can hopefully better understand themselves and the world around them.

*Create*—I love creativity! It's something new, different, and unique—whether it's in the form of words, art, film, stories, business, or nature. It's seeing what everyone sees but thinking what no one has thought. Creativity brings life and is a way of honoring God as the Creator.

*Relate*—If it doesn't involve others, what's the point? Everything

I do needs to be infused with others, even if it's during the times I'm thinking and creating. I will spend my time, talent, and treasure on the face in front of me and on those around me.

*Give*—Generosity needs to infuse everything I do. I will live my life with openness and a belief that I don't own it, so I don't need to hold on to it. I won't be owned by anything other than my purpose, and I will be open to giving away everything.

*Move*—I can't help it; I like to be on the move. All the questions—what is around the corner, what does that look like, how does that taste—need answers! I will stay in motion so that I can engage with the world in healthy and positive ways.

# Endnotes

Author's Note: The endnotes below are a compilation of references to source material, additional information that didn't necessarily fit within the body of the main text, as well as random non sequiturs or attempts at humor that may end up only being interesting or entertaining to myself but were nevertheless fun to add along the way.

1   See "No One Can Explain Why Planes Stay in the Air," *Scientific American*, Ed Regis, February 1, 2020.

2   In 2020, the trustees of the trust established by Gail elected to sell a majority interest in the Jazz to Ryan Smith, a Utah resident, lifelong Jazz fan and founder of Qualtrics. In Smith, Gail and the family saw someone else with the heart and head of a steward as well as someone who could help continue the purpose and legacy for which the trust was established and carry that on into the future. During the announcement of the part-sale, Gail recalled the thoughts and emotions behind the original acquisition some thirty-five years

prior and noted, "We were young and full of excitement at the prospect of being stewards of a unique asset and sharing it with Utah and beyond."

3 As may come as no surprise, the city of Cincinnati is actually named after Cincinnatus.

4 The Melians, despite their circumstances, refused to pay tribute to Athens or to take sides. After a six-month siege of the island nation, the Melians surrendered, and the Athenians put the male soldiers to death, sold the women and children as slaves, and ultimately colonized and took over the island for themselves.

5 https://msa.maryland.gov/msa/mdstatehouse/html/gwresignation.html

6 The phrase "Don't bury your talents!" derives from this parable.

7 Dr. Seuss, *Horton Hears A Who!* (New York: Random House, 1954).

8 I personally do not have a first-place medal from the Hawaii Ironman. I do, however, have a finisher medal from a short yet painful sprint triathlon I competed in several years ago. After nearly drowning in the man-made lake, enduring horrible leg cramps trying to get my wet suit off, and then gasping for air during the run portion of the race, I traded my tiny Speedo for spandex bike gear and never looked back.

9 https://medium.com/incerto/what-do-i-mean-by-skin-in-the-game-my-own-version-cc858dc73260

10 Nassim Nicholas Taleb, *Skin in the Game: Hidden Asymmetries in Daily Life* (New York: Random House, 2018).

11 https://www.goodreads.com/quotes/887640-the-important-thing-is-this-to-be-ready-at-any

12 https://kinginstitute.stanford.edu/king-papers/documents/suffering-and-faith

[13]   Harper Lee, *To Kill a Mockingbird* (New York: Harper Perennial Modern Classics, 2006).

[14]   https://www.rd.com/culture/most-used-noun-in-english/

[15]   Incidentally, the most used adjective is the word *good*, which beat out *bad* (thank goodness) and even *important*. The most used verb is actually *be*. As you might have guessed, the most used word is the word *the*, followed by the word *to*. The most used noun is *time*. Maybe we are trying to tell ourselves something, because if we combine the most used types of words together, we are saying, "The Time to be good."

[16]   Adrian Bejan, "Why the Days Seem Shorter as We Get Older," *European Review* (Published online by Cambridge University Press March 18, 2019).

[17]   https://knowledge.wharton.upenn.edu/article/time-vs-money-analyzing-which-one-rules-consumer-choices/

[18]   https://neilpatel.com/blog/5-psychological-studies/

[19]   Yes, okay, I admit it: I am that author. But the statement is also true. One of the things I enjoy the most is public speaking, and on more than one occasion, I have had people tell me, "You are just a natural on stage. I could never do that." The reality is that when I first started speaking in public, I would get so nervous my face would literally twitch, which in turn would make me even more nervous. The first time I delivered a "professional" presentation (to the Estate Planning Law Section of the Utah State Bar), I was so nervous I wrote it out line by line and read it without looking up once. The comfort I feel on a stage today is the result of countless hours spent on preparing, presenting, failing, and repeating.

[20]   https://www.salon.com/2016/04/10/malcolm_gladwell_got_us_wrong_our_research_was_key_to_the_10000_hour_rule_but_heres_what_got_oversimplified/

[21]   Ibid.

22  If you can't tell by now, I am AAA² ("all about alliteration" and "all about acronyms").

23  Ian Hathaway, "Almost half of Fortune 500 companies were founded by American immigrants or their children," Brookings Institution (December 4, 2017).

24  "The Demographics of Innovation in the United States," Adams Nager, David M. Hart, Stephen Ezell, Robert D. Atkinson (February 24, 2016).

25  Robert Arnott, William Bernstein, and Lillian Wu, "The Myth of Dynastic Wealth: The Rich Get Poorer," *Cato Journal* 35, no. 3 (2015): 447–485.

26  Avni M. Shah, Noah Eisenkraft, James R. Bettman, Tanya L. Chartrand, "'Paper or Plastic?': How We Pay Influences Post-Transaction Connection," *Journal of Consumer Research* 42, no. 5 (February 2016).

27  Ibid.

28  As a personal note, I come from a faith perspective that believes in a real, good, and knowable God who desires a relationship with each of us as individuals. That said, even if you also come from a perspective that believes in God or in a creator, I think it's important to think beyond your general concept of God to benefit from transcendence. Think about the characteristics of the god of your faith, whether that is justice, mercy, compassion, creativity, beauty, or any of a host of different values or descriptors. Believing in a god who has an innumerable number of values and characteristics can make it difficult for us finite creations to draw motivation and direction. By focusing on just a few characteristics of God that individually resonate with who you are as an individual, you have a much better chance of both experiencing God and emulating those qualities.

29  Frank White, *The Overview Effect—Space Exploration and Human Evolution* (Houghton-Mifflin, 1987).

30    https://www.facebook.com/nasaearth/posts/the-thing-that-really-surprised-me-was-that-it-earth-projected-an-air-of-fragili/10158089022322139

31    https://en.wikiquote.org/wiki/Yuri_Gagarin

32    https://www.sciencealert.com/a-major-psychological-effect-on-astronauts-in-orbit-could-be-essential-for-space-missions

33    https://www.thecut.com/2016/05/scientists-are-trying-to-solve-the-mystery-of-awe.html

34    https://positivepsychology.com/self-transcendence

35    https://www.psychologytoday.com/us/blog/the-meaningful-life/201908/viktor-frankl-and-the-statue-responsibility

36    https://www.cirquedusoleil.com/awe, see also https://www.vox.com/culture/2019/1/10/18102701/cirque-du-soleil-lab-of-misfits-neuroscience-awe

37    https://psycnet.apa.org/record/2012-16073-001

38    Cirque du Soleil. November 8, 2018. "Cirque du Soleil unlocks the mysteries of AWE Montreal."

39    2015 Characteristics of New Housing, US Census Bureau https://www.census.gov/newsroom/press-releases/2016/cb16-tps107.html

40    https://www.researchandmarkets.com/reports/4622689/self-storage-market-growth-trends-and

41    http://www.clinical-depression.co.uk/dlp/depression-information/major-depression-facts

42    Andrew T. Jebb, Louis Tay, Ed Diener, and Shigehiro Oishi, "Happiness, income satiation, and turning points around the world," *Nature Human Behaviour* 2 (2018): 33–38.

43  https://www.apa.org/news/press/releases/2018/01/perfectionism-young-people

44  https://www.independent.co.uk/life-style/perfectionism-suicide-link-study-body-kill-adolescents-western-ontario-mental-health-a7868581.html

45  https://kinginstitute.stanford.edu/king-papers/documents/unfulfilled-dreams

46  https://www.goodreads.com/quotes/14940-somehow-i-can-t-believe-that-there-are-any-heights-that

47  Michael A. Freeman, Paige J. Staudenmaier, Mackenzie R. Zisser, and Lisa Abdilova Andresen "The prevalence and co-occurrence of psychiatric conditions among entrepreneurs and their families," *Small Business Economics* 53 (2019): 323–342.

48  Carl Desportes Bowman, Jeffrey Dill, James Davison Hunter, *Culture of American Families: Executive Report*, Charlottesville, VA: Institute of Advanced Studies in Culture, University of Virginia, 2012.

49  Josephson Institute (2012). Josephson Institute's 2012 report card on the ethics of American youth.

50  Richard Weissbourd and Stephanie Jones, *The Children We Mean to Raise*, Making Caring Common Project, Harvard Graduate School of Education, 2014.

51  Elizabeth Cady Stanton *Eighty Years and More (1815–1897): Reminiscences of Elizabeth Cady Stanton*, (New York: T, Fisher Unwin 1898), 165.

52  The temperance movement, which was a movement to prohibit the sale of alcohol, was actually born from the women's rights movement. At the time, women had few, if any, legal or contractual rights, including the right to own and control property or obtain a divorce. Many women were trapped in abusive marriages with

alcoholic husbands who either refused to work or who squandered their resources. These women had little agency to leave these situations and, even if they were successful, they would often lose custody of their children to their former husbands. As a result, many women fought for the banning of the sale of alcohol as a means of potentially helping women in these situations.

53   Susan B. Anthony, "Fifty Years of Work for Woman," *Independent*, 52, (February 15, 1900).

54   Anthony was ultimately convicted of illegal voting and subject to a $100 fine, which she staunchly refused to pay. The judge ultimately backed down and didn't require Anthony to pay the fine.

55   Please note that I am taking no position on balanced dog training. The only thing I would recommend is to refrain from following the training method I employed to try to stop my dogs from barking when anyone dared to walk near our house, which was to simply yell at them and which has proved to be remarkably unhelpful.

56   One of the biggest debates in the scientific community with respect to the proposed space elevator is what bad music should be played as people travel in it.

57   For purposes of the analogy and to avoid drawing people into "bitter" epicurean battle lines that can easily be drawn, we will set aside a discussion of the merits of including umami in the essential elements of taste.

58   "The Psychology of Purpose," Adolescent Moral Development Lab at Claremont Graduate University for Prosocial Consulting and the John Templeton Foundation, February 2018.

59   Roy F. Baumeister, Kathleen D. Vohs, Jennifer L. Aaker, and Emily N. Garbinsky, "Some Key Differences Between a Happy Life and a Meaningful Life," *The Journal of Positive Psychology* 8, no. 6 (2013): 505–516.

60  https://quoteinvestigator.com/2014/11/29/purpose/

61  Daniel Coyle, *The Culture Code: The Secrets of Highly Successful Groups* (New York: Bantam Books 2018).

62  The story of the rich, young ruler can be found in the book of Mark 10:17–27.

63  https://www.becomingminimalist.com/clutter-stats/

64  Krista Garcia, "Minimalism Is Gaining Momentum, but Brands Shouldn't Fret Just Yet," eMarketer.com, September 5, 2018, https://www.emarketer.com/content/minimalism-is-gaining-momentum-but-brands-shouldn-t-fret-just-yet

65  Richard M. Piech, Daniela Strelchuk, Jake Knights, Jonathan V. Hjälmheden, Jonas K. Olofsson, Jane E. Aspell. "People with higher interoceptive sensitivity are more altruistic, but improving interoception does not increase altruism," *Scientific Reports* 7, no. 15,652 (2017).

66  Ibid.

67  Stephanie A. Hooker, Kevin S. Masters, Crystal L. Park, "A Meaningful Life is a Healthy Life: A Conceptual Model Linking Meaning and Meaning Salience to Health," *Review of General Psychology* 22, no.1 (2018).

68  Bruce W. Smith, Alex J. Zautra, "Purpose in Life and Coping with Knee-Replacement Surgery," *OTJR: Occupation, Participation, and Health*, January 1, 2000.

69  Amy Lee Ai, E. Mitchell Seymour, Terrence N. Tice, Ziad Kronfol, and Steven F. Bolling, "Spiritual struggle related to plasma interleukin-6 prior to cardiac surgery," *Psychology of Religion and Spirituality*, 1, no. 2, (2009): 112–128.

70  Ed O'Brien and Samantha Kassirer, "The Joy of Giving Lasts Longer Than the Joy of Getting," *Psychological Science,* (December 20, 2018).

71 "Sanduk Ruit: Everyone Deserves Good Vision," Ramon Magsaysay Award Foundation, July 25, 2016, https://www.rmaward.asia/rmtli/everyone-deserves-good-vision/

72 Sophie Brown, "Sight for sore eyes: 'Maverick' doctor who restored the vision of 100,000 people." CNN, accessed December 17, 2014, https://www.cnn.com/2014/12/14/world/asia/nepal-eye-doctor/index.html

73 In 1966, John Lennon proclaimed that the Beatles were more popular than Jesus, which provoked significant backlash at the time. Statistician Eric Schulman used a more analytical process to create a fame scale, which he has tabulated every few years since 2001. Jesus consistently ranks number one on his fame scale, though credit should go to the Beatles, who placed second. https://www.improbable.com/2016/08/29/who-is-the-most-famous-person-in-the-world-statistically

74 McKenna, Dave, "A Flair for the Absurd," *Washington City Paper*, April 2, 1999, https://washingtoncitypaper.com/article/273653/a-flair-for-the-absurd/

75 Martin B. Copenhaver, *Jesus is the Question: The 307 Questions Jesus Asked and the 3 He Answered* (Abingdon Press, 2014).

76 Hence why I think Jesus was in the transformation business and not the information business.

77 Again, the book *Riveted* by Andrew Howell and me is a great resource for understanding who you are, what you value, and what you believe.

78 Abraham H. Maslow, *Religions, Values and Peak-Experiences* (Columbus, Ohio: Ohio State University Press, 1964).

79 Timothy Keller, *Making Sense of God: An Invitation to the Skeptical* (Viking, 2016).

80 Ibid.

81   Unfortunately for them, the acronym for their values is LIE (which isn't great, especially if one of your values is integrity), but they decided to stick with it anyway.

82   Emily Esfahani Smith, *The Power of Meaning: Finding Fulfillment in a World Obsessed with Happiness* (Broadway Books, 2017).

83   Ibid.

84   While I definitely can't give you any additional time or talent, I could technically give you more money—but with five children, I really don't want to do that.

85   Martine Hennard Dutheil de la Rochère, Gillian Lathey, Monika Woźniak, *Cinderella Across Cultures: New Directions and Interdisciplinary Perspectives* (Wayne State University Press, 2016).

86   Rebecca Hickox and Will Hillenbrand, *The Golden Sandal: A Middle Eastern Cinderella Story* (Holiday House, 1999).

87   Daniel Coyle, *The Culture Code: The Secrets of Highly Successful Groups* (New York: Bantam Books 2018).

88   Boris Groysberg, Jeremiah Lee, Jesse Price, and J. Yo-Jud Cheng, "The Leader's Guide to Corporate Culture," *Harvard Business Review* (January–February 2018).

89   Ibid.

90   As my good friend Brad Fisher points out, listening may be the most transcendent gift of all.

91   Stephen R. Covey, *The 7 Habits of Highly Effective People: Restoring the Character Ethic* (New York: Free Press, 2004).

92   Albert V. Carron, Steven R. Bray, Mark A. Eys, "Team Cohesion and Team Success in Sport," *Journal of Sports Sciences* (December 9, 2010).

[93]   William E. Piper, Myriam Marrache, Renee Lacroix, Astrid M. Richardson, and Barry D. Jones, "Cohesion as a basic bond in groups," *Human Relations* 36, (1983): 93–108.

[94]   As a lifelong Utah Jazz fan, that may have been the hardest sentence I have ever had to write in my life. And let's just get this in print for posterity: Jordan pushed off (okay, he really didn't, but it sure felt like it at the time).

[95]   Daniel Coyle, *The Culture Code: The Secrets of Highly Successful Groups* (New York: Bantam Books, 2018).

[96]   http://positioningsystems.com/blog.php?entryID=67

[97]   Matthew A. Killingsworth and Daniel T. Gilbert, "A Wandering Mind Is an Unhappy Mind," *Science* 330, no. 6,006 (November 12, 2010): 932.

[98]   Ibid.

[99]   "How to Refocus the Wandering Mind? 6 Simple Ways," Meigan Sembrano, December 10, 2019, *The Jerusalem Post*

[100]  https://blogs.loc.gov/law/2013/03/frequent-reference-question-how-many-federal-laws-are-there/

[101]  I would like to thank Pastor Corey J. Hodges of the Point Church for pointing me to this quote and Professor Mecham's pillars in a great talk he gave on racism, reason, and hope.

[102]  https://www.thebipartisanpress.com/politics/historian-meacham-america-has-followed-the-devices-and-desires-of-white-peoples-hearts/

[103]  RBC 2017 Wealth Transfer Report

[104]  I've always loved that quote, and it is often used, but I have never been able to locate its original source.

[105]  Op. cit. RBC 2017 Wealth Transfer Report

106   2017 US Trust Insights on Wealth and Worth* survey of HNW individuals and families

107   David R. York and Andrew L. Howell, "GRATs or Gratitude? A New Type of Planning Is Needed to Meet 21st Century Demands," *Trusts & Estates*, May 2017, https://www.yorkhowell.com/resources/grats-or-gratitude/

108   For my ERISA savvy readers, you are correct. There is no such thing as a partner stock ownership plan and it is technically an employee stock ownership plan, but good luck telling the people at Bridgeway that fact.

109   More information on B Corporations can be found at www.bcorporation.net. A low-profit limited liability company (or LLLC) is the LLC corollary entity.

110   https://www.nerdwallet.com/article/investing/esg-investing

111   A fantastic resource for learning more about the Civilian Public Service can be found at www.civilianpublicservice.org.

112   Melvin Gingerich, *Service for Peace, A History of Mennonite Civilian Public Service* (Mennonite Central Committee, 1949).

113   Leah M. Kalm, Richard D. Semba, "They Starved So That Others Be Better Fed: Remembering Ancel Keys and the Minnesota Experiment," *The Journal of Nutrition* 135, no. 6, (June 2005).

114   SCORE Association (www.score.org).

115   United States Census Bureau.

116   *Forbes* magazine, 2015.

117   Ronald C. Anderson, David M. Reeb, "Founding-Family Ownership and Firm Performance: Evidence from the S&P 500," *The Journal of Finance* 58, no. 3 (June 2003).

118   Family Business Survey, 2016.

119   United States Department of Commerce

120   Barclays Wealth and the Economist Intelligence Unit, "Family Business: in Safe Hands?" Barclays Wealth Insights, Volume 8, 2009.

121   Gallo, Taples, & Cappuyns, 2004.

122   Calvi-Reveyron, 2000.

123   Lyagoubi, 2006.

124   PricewaterhouseCoopers 2014 Survey.

125   SCORE Association.

126   PricewaterhouseCoopers 2014 Survey.

127   Roy Williams and Vic Preisser, *Philanthropy, Heirs & Values: How Successful Families Are Using Philanthropy to Prepare Their Heirs for Post-Transition Responsibilities* (Robert Reed Publishers, 2010).

128   Ibid.

129   "Playing their hand: US family businesses make their bid for the future," US Family Business Survey, PricewaterhouseCoopers, 2012.

130   Bain & Company, 2014

131   Daniel Coyle, *The Culture Code: The Secrets of Highly Successful Groups* (New York: Bantam Books, 2018).

132   George G. Gordon and Nancy DiTomaso, "Predicting Corporate Performance, Organizational Culture," *Journal of Management Studies* 29, no. 6 (1992).

133   As noted earlier, the elements of belonging, purpose, transcendence, and story are found in the book *The Power of Meaning* by Emily Esfahani Smith.

CPSIA information can be obtained
at www.ICGtesting.com
Printed in the USA
BVHW040224060622
638991BV00002B/15